PHYSICALISM

STUDIES IN
PHILOSOPHICAL PSYCHOLOGY

Edited by
R. F. HOLLAND

PHYSICALISM

by
K. V. WILKES

HUMANITIES PRESS

ATLANTIC HIGHLANDS, N. J.

First published in 1978
by Humanities Press Inc.
Atlantic Highlands, N. J. 07716

Set in Times by
Computacomp (UK) Ltd., Fort William, Scotland
and printed in Great Britain by
Lowe & Brydone Printers Ltd., Thetford, Norfolk

Library of Congress Cataloging in Publication Data
Wilkes, K. V.
Physicalism.

(Studies in philosophical psychology)
Portions based on the author's thesis, Princeton, 1974.
Includes bibliographical references and index.
1. Psychology—Philosophy. 2. Mind and body.
I. Title. II. Series.
BF38.W74   150'.19'2   77-28169
ISBN 0 391 00741 6

CONTENTS

TO MY PARENTS

CHAPTER 1

RELATIONS AND RELATA

TO begin with an outstanding banality: the mind-body problem is the problem of the relationship between mind and body. This platitude has the single merit of making explicit the fact that we have here a two-termed relation, which may be schematised as 'aRb'; in which 'a' stands for whatever 'mind' stands for, 'b' does the same for 'body', and 'R' is proxy for the relation or relations that hold between the two. We have then on the face of it three candidate objects of study: each of the relata, and the relationship itself. Although it is the relationship that has borne the main brunt of philosophical investigation, we may find that it is as difficult to pin-point genuine relata as it is to disentangle the nature of the links holding between them.

At the outset, it is clear that the terms 'mind' and 'body' are themselves stand-ins for something more explicit. They are summarising labels; and what they summarise are normally taken to be, on the one hand, mental, and on the other, physical, events, states, and processes. Supposing, then, that these are the relata, how clear are they? For our present purposes the scope of the term 'physical' is relatively unproblematic. All we need say about it at the moment is that the expression 'the physical' picks out all and only the items, processes, concepts, laws, hypotheses, theories, or theoretical postulates used essentially by physical scientists. Any concept, therefore, which plays some significant role in a theory belonging to the physical sciences is *eo ipso* a physical concept. This means that it is no business of the philosopher layman to predict or restrict the conceptual elements in the framework of a science: he must accept as 'physical' whatever the physical scientist says is such. Certainly the philosopher of science may need to query or challenge various features of the theory, including elements of its conceptual apparatus. But the philosophy of physics is not our present concern: just now we should simply note that the scope of 'the physical' is the physical scientist's business.

On the physical side of the mind-body relation, then, there seems no bar in principle to the suggestion that the physical sciences which study the brain and human activity can have or devise a vocabulary adequate for the identification of any physical event, state, or process. We shall return eventually to a more detailed and comprehensive view of the physical; for the moment this will suffice. What of the other term of the relation, 'the mental'? This is much less clear. Unlike the physical, which can as we have seen be strictly delimited by the rather blank consideration that all and only the terms featuring essentially in the description of physical theories count as 'physical', the mental cannot be clearly described in a correspondingly neat manner. We have an intuitive idea of the range of the notion, derived from our regular everyday handling of many of the terms which comprise the category — but is there not something more clear-cut than intuition?

It would be easy and tempting to object at this point that there is no need to search for any criterion of the mental. Intuition alone would serve quite well: we tend to agree, after all, about what are and what are not mental terms. Indeed there might be *no* criterion to distinguish the mental from the non-mental, and yet this would present no obstacle either to the validity of the term 'mental' or to our claim of mastery over the concept: this has been conclusively established by Wittgenstein's discussion of family-resemblance terms. Now this objection is persuasive. It must be granted that we can handle mental terms with adequate facility, and usually have little doubt about our classification of phenomena as mental or not. Nevertheless the suggestion that we should rely exclusively upon intuition and convention to delimit the scope of the mental will not do, for the following reasons:

(1)   First and most powerfully, there may prove to be no worth-while or valid distinction at all to be drawn between mental and physical; in other words, the dichotomy may be a false one. However implausible this suggestion may seem at first sight, it is one aim of this work to exploit it; to make it more palatable now, I shall simply assert that the Greeks have no such cleavage – had nothing even approximately equivalent to it (see chapter 7).

(2)   Although we have a sure mastery of most mental concepts most of the time, we may be at a loss if required to label as 'mental' or 'non-mental' some very common and everyday terms. Several seem to hover in between mental and physical status, being a bit of both: 'nervous', 'asleep', 'unconscious' or 'dazed' are examples of predicates which are not clearly mental rather than physical, nor *vice versa*. Similarly, although 'thinking' seems indisputably mental, what of 'concluding' or 'contradicting'? We should rightly become impatient if pressed to give a definite answer to the question 'Mental or not?' asked of such terms; but to avoid such tedious questioning successfully, it would help to be able to say what is significant and essential about clearly mental concepts, and hence to explain what is – or isn't – mental about these apparent hybrids.

(3)   Everyday mental concepts are not the only ones with

which we must deal. The advance of the psychological sciences has opened up a wide and rough terrain of disputable cases. Drives; stimulus inputs; information retrieval mechanisms; the id-ego-superego triad; libido; unconscious, subconcious, and preconscious events and processes – any terms such as these will be tricky and perplexing to one seeking to delimit the mental by intuition, resisting neat (or even rough) categorisation as mental or non-mental.

(4)   We are already attributing to computers a large number of mentalistic concepts; add a dash of science fiction, and we find machines to which we may need to attribute yet more. Now even if we insist – for whatever reason – that a computer cannot add, but can only 'add', or, in short, that whatever mental term ϕ we take, computers can only ' ϕ ' and never ϕ, we need to justify our use of the insulating quotation marks. And to justify them, we would have to say what it is about human ϕ -ing that is missing from computer ' ϕ -ing'; that is, we must explain what is peculiarly mental about ϕ -ing. If on the other hand we were to allow that computers can indeed ϕ without the insulating quotes, then we can pertinently be asked why ϕ -ing is after all to be considered a mental rather than a physical process; this might return us to the first argument in reply to the objection: namely, is the mental – physical dichotomy really genuine?

Thus all things considered it seems necessary to try to characterise the mental more definitively; and if the attempt ends in failure, this too will be instructive and important. In fact there are available two popular theses, each of which is said to distinguish the mental from the physical.

The first of them, which I shall for convenience label 'the incorrigibility thesis', draws the distinction in terms of our special epistemological position *vis-à-vis* our mental events. It claims that mental phenomena are such that whoever has them is immediately aware of them; that they are private to their owner so that he has a privileged access to them; in short, that we are incorrigible about our own mental events in the sense that nobody could conceivably be thought mistaken if ever he sincerely asserted that he was, or was not, experiencing a particular mental phenomenon. This line of thought has been highly popular ever since Descartes.

There are two main flaws which mar any formulation of the incorrigibility thesis. The first, which will be discussed in greater detail later, is due to the vagueness and ambiguity of the terms used. Ayer has picked out no less than four senses of 'private',[1] and there may be more;[2] and none of these interpretations of the term, on examination, can justify or explain our alleged incorrigibility in respect of the private entities. 'Immediate awareness' is a notion which has been forcibly attacked by many discussions of sense-datum theories; and it looks extremely unlikely that we can characterise the objects of this special awareness in non-circular fashion – the objects of immediate awareness are just those things we are incorrigible about, and we are incorrigible about all and only the objects of immediate awareness. The kind of incorrigibility in question cannot be elucidated independently of these other suspect notions.[3] Nevertheless, we need not now linger over this particular flaw of the incorrigibility thesis: we shall be returning to it, and there is another difficulty which is clearer yet. The second drawback to the thesis is that the characterisation of the mental it suggests leaves out much that by intuition and common sense we would unhesitatingly include in the category. One who is self-deceived, for example, must be credited with beliefs and desires to which he would not admit he subscribed – we cannot make sense of the fact of self-deception otherwise. Again, the suggested criterion fails to cope with some emotions like anger – one can furiously but sincerely deny one is angry. The thesis further excludes moods and dispositions such as vanity, generosity, irritability and the like – for often we have no immediate awareness of these but, on the contrary, may be the last to realise we are vain, generous, or irritable. Moreover, it debars from mental status all preconscious, subconscious, and unconscious mental states or events. Perhaps most tellingly of all, it even excludes some mental phenomena which are conventionally seen as very paradigms of this criterion. Pains and after-images are popular illustrations of phenomena of which we are infallibly and immediately aware – yet there have recently appeared convincing arguments to suggest that it can make excellent sense to talk of pains of which one is not aware,[4] and certainly I may be unaware of an after-image if I am looking at a wall of the same shade against which it is invisible.

In sum, the incorrigibility thesis makes one rather imprecise point about many mental happenings, which needs considerable clarification and qualification before it is accepted: that the one who has the mental state in question often also has a privileged epistemological position in relation to it. But it cannot serve to give us any criterion of the mental.

The second view purporting to mark off the mental from the physical I shall call 'the intensionality thesis'. It may be useful to give a rough outline of what intensionality is before assessing the thesis. We can select three main criteria for distinguishing intensional from non-intensional sentences:

(A)   The first criterion treats sentences whose main verb takes a direct object. Such a sentence is intensional if the existence or non-existence of the item picked out by the direct-object phrase makes no difference to the truth values either of the sentence itself, or its negation. For example, 'The Greeks worshipped Zeus', and 'The Christians worship Jesus Christ', and the negations of those sentences, are alike true or false quite independently of any judgments we may make about the existence of Zeus or Jesus; so is 'Pooh hunted hippogriffs'. But 'The Jews crucified Jesus Christ', and 'Pooh caught a hippogriff' are not intensional sentences; for they would be falsified by the non-existence of Jesus Christ or hippogriffs.

(B)   The second criterion treats sentences whose main verb governs a propositional clause. Such a sentence will be intensional if the truth value of the contained sentence does not affect the truth values of the containing sentence and its negation. For example, 'Pooh hopes that a hippogriff will fall into his trap', and 'The Trojans believed that the wooden horse was harmless' are intensional by this criterion; the truth values of 'A hippogriff will fall into Pooh's trap', and 'The wooden horse was harmless' may vary without varying the truth values of the whole sentences. But 'It is true that the wooden horse was harmless', and 'It is a fact that Pooh caught a hippogriff' are not intensional; both are falsified by the falsity of the contained propositions.

(C)   The third criterion treats sentences with main verbs of either kind. Take any set of pairs of descriptions in which each pair denotes the same thing; and take any sentence where the object of the verb, whether direct or propositional, includes in its description one member of such a pair. Then a sentence is intensional if the substitution of the other member of the pair for the first may affect the truth values of the complete sentence and its negation. Suppose that the expression 'the wooden horse', and 'the booby-trap prepared by the Greeks to take Troy' pick out the same object. Then although 'The Trojans believed the wooden horse was harmless' is probably true, 'The Trojans believed that the booby-trap prepared by the Greeks to take Troy was harmless' is certainly false. The truth value of non-intensional sentences, however, remains unaffected by such substitutions; they all obey the compelling principle that reference-preserving substitutions in a sentence preserve its truth value. Hence, if 'Cicero denounced Catiline' is true, then so must be 'Cicero denounced a man who was praetor in 68 BC.'

These three criteria spell out what Brentano called the 'Intentional Inexistence' of mental phenomena, such as believing, wishing, hoping, fearing, and the like;[5] their objects, whether substantial or propositional, need not exist or be the case in the real world. To use intensionality as a mark of the mental is to make the claim that whenever we are describing or explaining mental phenomena we have to use intensional sentences, whereas when we are describing physical phenomena any intensional sentence we happen to use will prove eliminable.

Now intensionality is not wholly adequate as a mark of the mental. Some intensional sentences are clearly non-mental — notoriously those involving modal operators, like 'It is possible that p', and 'It is necessarily true that p'. Conversely, some clearly mental sentences do not fit the thesis very readily: 'John has a pain' is not itself obviously intensional, and it is unclear that it must emerge as intensional even under a fuller description or explanation (it is interesting that the mental phenomena claimed to fit the incorrigibility thesis best, fit the intensionality thesis least well, and *vice versa*). Nevertheless, with a few such qualifications, we should admit that intensionality is a feature of a great number of sentences ascribing mental states to people; and this feature, as we shall discover, is one of immense significance to the exploration of the mind-body relation.

Thus, although we have found no single adequate criterion of what it is to be mental, we have progressed somewhat. We can note that many mental phenomena are such that their owner is in a privileged epistemological position in relation to them; and that yet more have the peculiarity that intensional sentences are required to ascribe or describe them. These two theses, combined with our intuitions about what is mental and what is not, will suffice for the moment as a seemingly tolerable delineation of the category that is to be related to the physical. Later on, we shall discover more telling objections to the whole notion of 'the mental'.

With something said about the terms of the relation, we can now turn to the relation itself. Many candidate relations have been proposed; here follows a list (incomplete) of some of the mind-body connections for and against which philosophers have argued:

(a) M (the mental) is identical with P (the physical). (The Identity Theory.)

(b) M is nothing but P. ('Nothing-but' materialism.)

(c) M runs parallel with P. (Parallelism.)

(d) M causally interacts with P. (Interactionism.)

(e) M is an emergent property of P. (Emergentism.)

(f) M is not required in explanation, P is. (Behaviourism.)

(g) M-explanations can be reduced to, or paraphrased into, P-explanations. (Reductionism.)

(h) Descriptions of M pick out functional states of the structures picked out by P-descriptions. (Functionalism.)

(The labels used here are not important, and are introduced simply for ease of reference.)

We can see from this list that the relations in question fall into two significantly distinct types. One type, (a) − (e), states or implies something about what the mental is − the concern is ontological; the second, (f) − (h), centres around questions of explanation. This distinction will be so crucial for the subsequent discussion that it requires clear explanation.

One might be interested in the question what mental states, events, and processes precisely are. In particular, are they the same as, or radically distinct from, physical events, states, and processes (where 'physical' is given the interpretation discussed above)? The primary thrust of such an inquiry is towards some ontological conclusion: how many kinds of thing there are. Alternatively, one might be more intrigued by the following query: no matter what mental phenomena may prove to be, do we need to make ineliminable reference to them when explaining behaviour? The primary thrust of this inquiry is scientific; it asks whether the vocabulary and theories of physical sciences are adequate to describe, predict and explain the purposive behaviour of humans and animals, as we trust they are adequate to describe and explain the behaviour of inanimate matter. I shall call the first, or ontological, question the issue of monism; the second, or scientific, question is the issue of physicalism.

Now just as we have two distinct topics, so we get distinct problems besetting each of them. For example, monists who are identity theorists have to decide whether they want to defend a strict Leibnizian identity between mental and physical, or a looser theoretical identity; whether this is to hold between mental and physical items (pains, brain states) or mental and physical properties (having a pain, being in a certain brain state); whether the identities hold generally or are merely particular identities; and whether the identity is necessary or contingent. (We learn much about the concept of identity from this debate.) All monists and dualists, of whatever types, are confronted with the question of evidence: how might their theses be established? Physicalists, in their turn, have the problem of picking their way along a *via media* between the Scylla of behaviourism and the Charybdis of intensionality. Few people now have much faith in radical behaviourism, which claims *inter alia* that behaviour can be described and explained with no reference whatever to non-physical terms (and savagely restricts even the physical terms to be used in explanation); but as soon as one allows in non-physical concepts such as desire, belief and the like, and then seeks to translate them into, reduce them to, or explain them by, physical terms, there arises the major difficulty of the apparent non-equivalence of an intensional sentence to any extensional (non-intensional) one.

A third difference exists between the two issues. Earlier we saw that there were two prevalent theses which offered to characterise 'the mental'. The incorrigibility thesis picked out best the sensation-type mental phenomena: pains, itches, tingles, twitches, images, after-images, sense impressions. Such things, with the exception perhaps of sense impressions, seem relatively easy to individuate and count – the idea is that they tend to be clockable, occurrent, phenomenal. The intensionality thesis, on the other hand, fits such mental happenings rather poorly, but does, as the incorrigibility thesis does not, pick out the propositional attitudes of belief and desire, expectation, fear, memory, thought. Now the propositional attitudes are extremely difficult to identify or count (as will be discussed at greater length in the next chapter). They are, however, to a much greater extent than occurrent sensations, our major source for explanations of behaviour – to understand an action, we want to know what the agent wanted, believed, expected, and the like. Consequently it is between datable and individuatable, occurrent sensations that monism or dualism are generally (but not invariably[6]) argued to hold; while physicalists and their opponents are much more concerned with the explanatory intensional concepts of belief, desire, *et al*.

A fourth difference lies in the consequences of philosophical research into these two clusters of problems. The debate over the truth of monism holds little interest for science, and science has little to say to it; but physicalism is itself a debate about and for science. To see this, consider how the truth of monism might be established. Not, clearly, by any evidence unearthed by neurophysiologists. For there is no evidence for, say, an identification of a sensation with a brain process that is not also and equally evidence for their parallelism; conversely, no scientific findings could refute any monistic theory without thereby refuting parallelism, emergentism, or most prevalent dualist theses. It is only interactionism – never a very plausible or popular dualist thesis – which might be supported or refuted by neurophysiological research if, for instance, gaps in the chain of physical causality were discovered or denied. Nor can we say that science is relevant to monism in that considerations of scientific economy require us to use Occam's Razor to cut mental phenomena out of our ontology, and hence require us simply to *assert* that any law-like 'correlations' we may have found between mental and physical should be regarded as identifications. For such ontological economising would in fact achieve no scientific economy at all – evidently there would be precisely as many laws of identity between the mental and the physical as there were formerly laws of correlation.[7] (Moreover, note that the dualist is unlikely to succumb willingly to the Razor. He has at the outset explicitly declared himself in favour of a rich ontology and an *un*simple view of the relation of the mental to the physical, and so will be unimpressed by arguments urging the demands of scientific parsimony.)

Physicalism, on the other hand, concerns scientists obviously and vitally. If we failed to describe or explain the behaviour of people in physical terms, then there would be a class of events which escapes the nomological net of the physical sciences; moreover, a vast amount of contemporary psychophysiological research would prove to be fundamentally misguided. Indeed this may be so: but clearly the question is important.

In the following chapters I shall be explicitly discussing the topic of physicalism. However, while examining the problem and offering a solution, we shall bring in considerations which will prepare the way for some answer to the issue of monism. A brief promissory note: as hinted earlier, my solution will make central use of the idea that the mental-physical dichotomy is not nearly as interesting as it is thought to be.

Notes

1 'Privacy', in A.J. Ayer, *Concept of a Person and Other Essays* (London, 1963), pp. 52–81.
2 Castañeda finds six senses of 'private object'; see H.-N. Castañeda, 'The Private Language Argument as a *Reductio ad Absurdum*', in O. R. Jones (ed.), *The Private Language Argument* (London, 1971), p. 137.
3 Rorty has discussed the notion of incorrigibility and has clarified a defensible sense of it while attacking the sense with which I am here concerned; see R. Rorty, 'Cartesian Epistemology and Changes in Ontology', in J.E. Smith (ed.), *Contemporary American Philosophy*, Second Series (London, 1970), pp. 273–92.
4 See G. Pitcher, 'Pain Perception', *Philosophical Review*, LXXIX (1970), pp. 368–93.
5 Franz Brentano, *Psychologie vom empirishen Standpunkte* (Leipzig, 1924), vol. I, pp. 124f.
6 Davidson argues for monism, at the expense of physicalism, and employs the intensionality thesis of the mental in offering a proof of monism. However, it is significant that the refutation of physicalism is the main point of his paper. See D. Davidson, 'Mental Events', in L. Foster and J.W. Swanson (eds). *Experience and Theory* (Massachusetts, 1970), pp. 79–101.
7 Kim argues this point more fully and convincingly. See J. Kim, 'On the Psycho-Physical Identity Theory', *American Philosophical Quarterly*, III (1966), pp. 227–35.

CHAPTER 2

INTENSIONALITY AND IRREDUCIBILITY

WE saw in the last chapter that intensionality, although inadequate as a general criterion of the mental, did serve to mark out a large and important class of mental sentences; in particular, it picked out those sentences that ascribe just the mental states most typically used in the everyday explanation of behaviour. For example, all the following verbs create intensional sentences: believe, think, remember, wish, want, will, reason, decide, plan, choose, assess, weigh up, intend, hope, fear, expect, regret, resolve; be ashamed or proud of, embarrassed or grateful for — and the list could continue indefinitely. Yet more verbs can be used in both intensional and extensional sentences; if John mistakes a bush for a bear, it is in order to say both 'John saw a bush' (extensional), and (although perhaps less naturally) 'John saw a bear' (intensional) — in fact whenever 'see' is used in what we may call its 'seeing-as' sense, the sentence used will be intensional.[1] Various other verbs may seem *prima facie* to leave their sentences untainted by intensionality: 'He is depressed' looks extensional enough. But such sentences contain a latent intensionality, in that a fuller description and explanation of the phenomenon requires the use of explicitly intensional sentences. To explain his depression we may use sentences such as: 'Things look black to him', or 'He is taking a pessimistic view of everything'. This latent intensionality probably marks most, if not all, sentences ascribing moods, dispositions, and emotions; and these are phenomena frequently cited in the ordinary explanations of actions. The mental sentences which seem entirely free of intensionality are, by and large, far less central to the description and explanation of behaviour than those listed here.

Before discussing the problem posed to physicalism by the fact of intensionality, I shall introduce two terminological innovations. The first is to extend the use of the predicate 'intensional' so that it can be a predicate of items other than sentences; this will avoid clumsy and long-winded locutions. I extend it by calling the main verb of an intensional sentence an intensional verb; and the cognate noun or noun-phrase will pick out an intensional concept. Hence 'believe' will be an intensional verb, and 'belief' introduces the intensional concept of belief. Further, the object of an intensional verb, be it a direct or a propositional object, I shall call an intensional object, and the description which gives this object will be an intensional description. Hence, in the intensional sentences 'John wants a banana', and 'John believes that pigs can fly', 'wants' and 'believes' are intensional verbs, wanting and belief are intensional concepts, 'a banana' and 'pigs can fly' are intensional descriptions introducing their intensional objects, *viz.* a banana and the proposition that pigs can fly. Finally, verbs, concepts, descriptions, and objects may all be latently intensional, in the sense described above.

The second terminological short cut is to abbreviate the list of physical sciences concerned with the study of the brain and central nervous system — neurophysiology, neuroanatomy, biochemistry, biology, mechanics, and the like — to the single term 'neurophysiology', which should therefore be understood to mean 'neurophysiology and all the other sciences devoted to the study of the brain and central nervous system'.

Now we should try to formulate the notorious problem presented to physicalism by the fact of intensionality. Precise formulation is not easy, but from the following argument we will be able to grasp the central difficulty. The argument runs: physicalism is the attempt to explain purposive human behaviour in the terminology of the physical sciences. The physical sciences are wholly extensional. Hence any intensional terms that might be employed in the description or explanation of human action must be eliminated at some stage: reduced to, or explained or paraphrased by, extensional sentences. And this is impossible: no extensional sentence, or set of such sentences, ever has the same truth-conditions as an intensional sentence. But actions cannot be identified without recourse to intensionality; and as for their explanation, this too is impossible without intensionality. Hence neither the description nor the explanation of action can be given in purely extensional terms.

This claim is so general that its statement has to remain somewhat imprecise. For example, how are we to understand 'explain' in the phrase 'the attempt to explain purposive human behaviour' above? The answer will depend on how ambitious we take physicalism to be: it may seek to provide extensional sentences whose truth is necessary, or sufficient, or both, for the attribution of actions. The question of just what it does seek to provide must remain open, for the interpretations of physicalism vary, and we must continue to discuss whether intensionality can be eliminated without assuming a single interpretation. Hence the vague locutions 'reduced to, or explained or paraphrased by' above. A second sort of imprecision: what are the 'actions' that we are describing and explaining? In the standard discussions of physicalism, they are usually such events as signing one's name, putting up an umbrella, crossing the street — the ordinary actions that we explain in everyday life by ascribing certain beliefs and desires to the agent. But it is notoriously difficult to identify 'an action' precisely: and the lack of any sharp distinction between describing and explaining actions compounds the problem. As we know well, actions can be described with more or less detail or generality; one action description may include what in another counts as the circumstances or the consequences. The difference between 'Jones shot Smith' and 'Jones killed Smith' is that what was a consequence of the former becomes included as part of the action in the latter; the difference between 'Jones killed Smith' and 'Jones murdered Smith' is that the second includes what for the first were circumstances – the circumstances that make a killing a murder. Now this is a familiar enough problem, and latitude in event description is not unique to the theory of action. The point is worth mentioning for its connection with another familiar point: it is impossible to distinguish an action description from an action explanation. Suppose we have two descriptions of an action, D and D', where D' is fuller (more detailed, or including more of what for D were circumstances or consequences). Then it will often happen that D' will serve to explain D. 'Why is he signing his name?' A fuller description may explain: 'He is writing a cheque.' Again, 'Why is he writing a cheque for £50,000?', and the explanatory answer, 'He is ransoming his daughter from a kidnapper.' It seems entirely arbitrary whether we prefer to explain an action by giving it a fuller description or by resorting to the explicit vocabulary of explanation, 'Because he wants to ransom his daughter from a kidnapper and thinks that £50,000 will do it.' Now *this* point, too, is not worth stressing in isolation. But when added to the first observation – that actions are amenable to being described on various levels of generality and detail – we find a fairly extreme latitude in the choice of action description which makes it difficult to identify the physicalist's *explanandum*, and hence his *explanans*. Certainly no science is free of this latitude; any event may be variously described and, in any sphere, describing more fully may count as explaining. Nevertheless, within the tight framework of a developed science, the theory of that science will determine pretty exactly how and where event descriptions are to be limited, and what, in context, counts as *explanandum* and what as *explanans*; and physicalism lacks any such framework. For the actions we are talking about are, apparently, the ordinary actions we meet with in everyday life, and the descriptions and explanations are those of common idiom. Thus there is a real problem, and one which makes it more complicated to formulate the difficulty presented by intensionality to physicalism. For some want to claim that it is the description of action that cannot be given without intensional terms; others may or may not want to claim this, but do claim that the explanation of actions in terms of beliefs and desires is not reducible to any non-intensional explanation. Thus, in assessing the difficulty, we shall have to discuss quite generally the question of the eliminability of intensionality at all levels of description or explanation. Let us, then, turn to scrutinise various theories that attempt to do away with it.

I − The most radical attempt to exclude intensionality is found in extreme behaviourism. It excludes it at the outset by allowing it no place at any point; actions are to be described in terms which refer to 'colourless bodily movements',[2] and the explanations are to be couched in terms of stimulus and response. If extreme behaviourism could indeed produce an adequate theory of human behaviour, then intensionality would evidently not be a problem after all; but it cannot. To say it cannot is not something that can be conclusively proved, but familiar arguments show behaviourism to be both implausible and unattractive. I shall cite two kinds of argument against behaviourism; one points to specific difficulties of the theory, the other gives reason for distrusting the whole enterprise of behaviourism at a more general level.

Specifically, then, we can see that behaviourism fails to explain or predict — maybe because it does not describe adequately — some of the very simplest behaviour of mice and men. A neat example of Dennett's amply illustrates this:[3]

> Suppose a mouse were trained, in a Skinner box with a food reward, to take exactly four steps forwards and press a bar with its nose; if Skinner's laws truly held between stimuli and responses defined in terms of bodily motion, were we to move the bar an inch further away, so four steps did not reach it, we would have to predict that the mouse would jab its nose into the empty air rather than take a fourth step.

Dennett adds that this unfortunate implication cannot be evaded by describing the action in terms of the result achieved — the bar getting depressed. For if one did that, it would become impossible to explain perceptual illusions. Pigeons, like men, can be fooled by the Müller-Lyer lines, and so we cannot describe their behaviour in terms of the result they have been trained to achieve, the selection of the longer of two sticks. Fooled by the Müller-Lyer illusion, they may peck at the shorter.

Now conceivably these difficulties, and others like them, can be ironed out by an ingenious and devoted behaviourist; perhaps a way can be found to describe actions in such a way that the behaviour of both the mouse and the pigeon can be explained, and without resorting to the intensional, or latently intensional, descriptions, 'The mouse walks to the bar', and 'The pigeon pecks at the stick which seems longer.' I suspect, but cannot prove, that every proposed remedy will carry its own disadvantages. But whatever conclusion we reach about such difficulties of detail, there are powerful general arguments against the whole behaviourist enterprise. First, it has had over fifty years in which to prove itself, in which to establish the claim that it is a fruitful methodology; and the positive results have been strikingly meagre. The very consistency of its lack of success betrays system in the failures — an inadequate theory. Second, its extreme poverty of theory surely dooms it from the outset. No theory which restricts itself to such a small and simple ontology and set of postulates could hope to explain anything as complex as human behaviour, when theories of far greater sophistication and complexity are required to account for the properties and behaviour of inanimate matter. Koch, a practising psychologist, sums up the case neatly: 'In my humble opinion, behaviourism is finished. If there is residual motility, it is only that the corpse does not understand my arguments'.[4]

I shall here leave the explicit discussion of behaviourism; its merits and demerits are assessed in a copious literature. But because behaviourism takes such a radical course in the attempt to avoid intensionality, any failures found in less drastic measures will tend to increase its implausibility; so in a sense it will remain under examination.

II — Without being a behaviourist in the extreme sense outlined above, one may yet share with behaviourists of that kind the view that actions can be described extensionally. Now to avoid any taint of intensionality, latent as well as explicit, this will entail describing behaviour as nothing but bodily movement. A bus driver who is signalling a right turn by stretching his arm through the window must be described as 'extending his arm', for 'signalling a right turn' is latently intensional; to signal is to express an intention to turn, a desire to convey information to other road users. The trouble with this suggestion is that one cannot achieve this extensional purity without changing the subject. Physicalism hopes to explain action, not merely movement; reflex bodily movements, such as the patellar jerk, present no problems. Thus it must be able to distinguish between an uncontrollable spasmodic movement on the part of the driver, and a voluntary action. But to do this, to make this distinction, we have to know what sort of action it is. With our bus driver, unless we smuggle in various intensional presuppositions, we cannot do this. The old joke runs that a little old lady behind the driver taps on the window and says, 'Keep both hands on the wheel, young man; I'll tell you when it's raining.' Now she identifies his action — incorrectly, certainly, but none the less she identifies it — as an action of weather-detecting; a latently intensional description. The point is that unless an action is given a latently intensional description, we do not know if we are talking of actions or not; to see something as an action is to see it as something done with a purpose. Hence the complete exclusion of latent intensionality from action description constitutes a change of subject; the descriptions are no longer *action* descriptions. This argument will receive further support from a claim to be argued below: that there is no non-arbitrary distinction that can be drawn between descriptions and explanations of actions.

III — A third strategy for coping with intensionality is one that tries to do without intensional terms like 'belief' and 'desire' in the explanation of action. It allows that action descriptions may be latently intensional, but insists that the explanations must not be — that any sentences ascribing beliefs and desires are eliminable. Now such a claim instantly runs into trouble because descriptions and explanations of action cannot readily be distinguished. Should we say, 'Jim entered a shop', and explain why he did so by citing a belief and a desire, 'because he wanted tobacco and believed they sold it there', then we would have a specific belief and desire to eliminate; but should we describe him as 'entering a shop in search of tobacco', that belief and that desire would have been tacitly absorbed into the action description, and others quite different will be required to account for his behaviour as newly descibed. Let us, however, sidestep this problem by taking as given a fairly bare action description such as the first, and examine the reducibility of whatever belief or desire we may use to explain it.

There are two possible ways of getting rid of these intensional verbs. One is to provide a set of counterfactuals, couched in purely extensional terms, saying what the agent would do or say if ..., a set which would, if satisfied, license the attribution to him of a particular belief or desire; the second is to search for a state of the brain which correlates in lawlike fashion with the belief or desire. I shall discuss them separately as IIIA and IIIB.

IIIA — This suggestion fails at once, but for interesting reasons. It fails because no belief or desire (or fear, hope, expectation, etc.) can be attributed to any agent unless we implicitly ascribe to him a further background consisting of a host of other beliefs, desires, and psychological traits of various kinds. Consequently no set of counterfactual conditionals, whether couched in purely extensional terms or not, will serve to license the ascription of a particular belief or desire unless just such a background is assumed for that set as well. The point is most easily illustrated if we consider actions which are so unusual or abnormal that we are unsure which of several feasible explanations to prefer. Suppose, for example, Jim climbs a tree in midsummer and carefully picks off the leaves, one by one. We might try to explain this by saying, 'He wants to paint the tree as it would look in winter', but to do this we have to assume he believes, *inter alia*, that the tree is deciduous and loses its leaves in winter; or we might suggest 'He believes that Martians have put spying devices in the leaves and wants to frustrate them' — and for this, clearly, we must suppose him to hold many bizarre beliefs, fears, and expectations about Martians; perhaps the explanation is 'He wants to eat the leaves', but even this relatively mundane solution presupposes that we are crediting him with odd gastronomic preferences or dietary beliefs. The point is that whatever explanation we eventually think the most likely will be selected as such because of many other beliefs, desires, and psychological traits with which we are prepared to credit him. Now with normal and everyday actions, of the sort we regularly perform ourselves or see others performing, the explanation is usually evident, and there are no equally plausible accounts to compete with it. In fact we take it for granted that the doer of an ordinary sort of action has just those familiar and predictable desires and beliefs that we have, or would have in his position; and the belief and desire we cite to explain his action fit naturally into them. We are content with the answer 'Because he thinks it is raining' to the question 'Why is he putting up his umbrella?' because we take it for granted that he, like many people much of the time, prefers to stay dry and believes that umbrellas serve that end. This belief and preference we do not need to make explicit, and so it is easy to forget that they must be there, if 'He thinks it is raining' is indeed to explain his putting up his umbrella. But on the other hand 'He thinks it is raining' will not explain his action if this is done indoors, unless we suppose a great deal that is abnormal or unusual about some of his other beliefs; and these we might need to make explicit.

Evidently, then, sets of counterfactual conditionals cannot be freed from this latent intensionality, this tacit or sometimes overt attribution of a complex psychological background.

Suppose we hope to eliminate the believing in 'He believes it is raining'. Of the counterfactuals we might try, take 'If he had an umbrella, he would put it up', or 'If someone uttered the sentence, "Do you think it is raining?" he would utter the word "Yes" (or nod his head, etc.).' Neither of these would be successful unless we assumed, for the first conditional, that he wanted to stay dry and believed that umbrellas keep the rain out; for the second, that he understands English, wants to answer honestly, believes that saying 'Yes' or nodding his head is a means of signifying assent, and so forth. In short, although it is an unimpeachable truism that beliefs and desires are attributed on the basis of behaviour, linguistic and non-linguistic, this truism needs supplementing: 'so long as we are also implicitly or explicitly ascribing to him a further bundle of psychological traits in the background, in conjunction with which the belief and desire do indeed explain the action in question.'

To put it crudely, beliefs and desires do not come individually wrapped, but are all tied up together. No desire or belief of whatever kind can ever be attributed in isolation; each needs a background of related desires and beliefs into which it fits, against which it can be seen as rational. Thus we can say, more simply still, that all our attributions presuppose a measure of rationality on the part of the agent; so if an action is to be explained by citing a belief or desire, that belief or desire must be such that, *for* the agent and *given* other beliefs and desires of his, it explains how the action seemed rational.

Nor is it possible to avoid this conclusion by trying to start completely from scratch − making no assumptions about rationality whatever, and ascribing no beliefs and desires at all − trying to build up for an agent a theory about his whole web of interlocking beliefs and desires, on the basis solely of what we see him doing. For we have no way of telling whether or not, once we have built such a theory, a completely incompatible theory might not serve to explain his behaviour as well or better; this point is evidently closely allied to the thesis of the indeterminacy of translation. Moreover, when we are choosing the constitutive elements of this web, we cannot but be guided by certain indispensable principles: that in general he will tend to believe what is true; that in general he will not tolerate inconsistent beliefs; that in general he will accept the obvious entailments of his beliefs; in short, that in general he is rational. This ineliminable presupposition of rationality, without which our enterprise could not even begin, brings with it an intensionality that pervades every description, interpretation, and explanation of human behaviour cast in terms of what an agent does, and what he would do if .... The attempt to evade intensionality by analysing beliefs and desires into sets of counterfactual conditionals cannot, therefore, succeed.

IIIB — The second suggested method of eliminating talk of beliefs, desires, and other such intensional states was to discover, for each of them, a state of the brain with which it was correlated in a lawlike manner; thus every belief, etc., could, once identified, be translated into its neurophysiological equivalent. Now from the discussion of IIIA above, we know that the attribution of a belief or desire to an agent will only be correct if a host of further ascriptions of psychological states are taken as correct. Consequently, if we are to identify any particular desire or belief before searching for its neurophysiological correlate, we must identify a great many more. This obstacle is perhaps not as yet significant or insuperable; it means that to obtain extensional purity we must provide extensional correlates for every psychological trait, which was no more than we intended to do in the first place. However, not all such traits will be readily individuated.

How are we to pick out a belief, a memory, a mood, and the like? We must select for these categories items which are unambiguously what they are, and which tolerate reidentification. Otherwise, lawlike correlations with the systematically classified items of neurophysiological theory will be impossible. Suppose we can attribute to Joe the belief that his train leaves at 3.00 p.m. This may look to be the same as the belief held by Jim, who is also hoping to travel on a 3.00 p.m. train. However, Joe is in Edinburgh, journeying to London; Jim is in London, journeying to Edinburgh. So Joe's belief may be that the train *to London* leaves at 3.00 p.m., which is emphatically not the same as Jim's belief. Which belief, then, should we actually attribute to Joe? The question seems both unreal and pointless. Examples can be multiplied indefinitely: Jack believes Cicero denounced Catiline, James, that Tully did – the same belief, or not? We cannot tell; and what is more, there seems little sense to the question. A problem of another sort: Jeremy is thinking about Vienna. How many thoughts is that? It is described as one; but he is, *inter alia*, thinking about the coffee-shops, the opera, the hotel he stayed in, and the architecture of Vienna. Again, there seems no sense to the 'How many?' question. John, for his part, is remembering Vienna. Is this the same as thinking about Vienna? Of course, memories are kinds of thought, but the reverse is not always true; and some beliefs count as memories too, although some do not. There is no non-arbitrary answer to a question of the form: 'Are we to call this a belief, a thought, a memory, an opinion, a prejudice, or what?' If this sort of question were not intractable enough, moods and emotions present an even worse-seeming difficulty; if Joseph and Jeremiah are both depressed or proud, are their mental states the same? We have to say: it depends. And what all such questions as these depend on is the context in which we are discussing the matter, our interests and purposes in making the attributions. There is no such thing as an objective answer to these difficulties, for the mental flux does not come ready-sliced. We can carve it up as we like; one sort of carving will give us very many mental states, another much fewer. I shall not labour the point here, for I am reverting to it in the next chapter; but its force should be noted.

There is yet another obstacle to the suggestion of IIIB. There seems no good reason to suppose that the neurophysiological state of two persons whom we have (somehow) credited with 'the same belief' will be the same, and such that we could read off from the brain state just what that belief is (as we would need to do if we are to eliminate statements about individual beliefs). For the firing patterns of neurons depends upon which neurons have fired just before, and upon what neural firing patterns have already been laid down in the brain, and presumably upon all sorts of further neurophysiological factors; thus there is every reason to suppose that no two brains will encode the same belief in the same way, and even to suppose that two occasions of, say, 'feeling pride' in one and the same brain may be recorded differently. And this would bring an abrupt end to our aspirations of finding neurophysiological correlates for brain states which correlate in any *lawlike* fashion with their counterparts. Put another way: it is as unlikely that there is a brain state, or disjunction of brain states, which correlates with depression (for example) as − to borrow an example of Taylor's[5] − that there is a set of conditions which correlates with the state: 'a bridge's being unsafe'. IIIA seems as fruitless as was IIIB.

All in all, things look bad for physicalists. The everyday descriptions and explanations of action resist all attempts to recast them in terms appropriate for the physical sciences, that is, in extensional terms; human behaviour resists capture in the nomological net of the physical sciences. Certain kinds of monism and dualism also are damaged by the arguments of this chapter – for example, a monist who seeks to defend general identities between intensional mental states and physical states will be deprived of the lawlike correlations he requires before he can assert any general identities, and the dualist who opts for a regular parallelism between intensional mental states and physical ones is equally frustrated. However, the problem is not so grave for monists and dualists as it is for physicalists. For the question of monism, I have argued, does not engage science; hence monists and dualists have no need to defend general identities or lawlike parallelisms, since particular or random correlations and parallelisms would serve. Further, the dispute over the truth of monism is usually conducted over mental states marked rather by incorrigibility than by intensionality, and so evades much of the difficulty. But physicalists must find some solution, or give up their project entirely.[6]

Notes

1 See G.E.M. Anscombe, 'The Intentionality of Sensation: A Grammatical Feature', in R.J. Butler (ed.), *Analytical Philosophy, Second Series* (Oxford, 1965), pp. 158–80.

2 C.L. Hull, *Principles of Behaviour* (New York, 1943), p. 25.

3 D.C. Dennett, 'Intentional Systems', *Journal of Philosophy*, LXVIII (1971), p. 98.

4 S. Koch, 'Psychology as Science', in S.C. Brown (ed.), *Philosophy of Psychology* (London, 1974), p. 4.

5 C. Taylor, 'Mind-Body Identity: A Side Issue?', *Philosophical Review*, LXXVI (1967), pp. 206–7.

6 For further discussion of the central theme of this chapter, see D. Davidson, 'Mental Events', in L. Foster and J.W. Swanson (eds), *Experience and Theory* (Massachusetts, 1970); and his article 'Psychology as Philosophy', in Brown, *op.cit.*

CHAPTER 3

PSYCHOLOGY AND 'PSYCHOLOGY'

ONE moral to draw from the discussion of the preceding chapter is that we should consider more carefully just what is involved in the project of physicalism. The bare and uninformative description we have used so far is this: physicalism seeks to explain the purposive behaviour of human beings in purely physical terms. This description proved unsatisfactory largely because of the vagueness of 'explain', and also because of the difficulty of picking out the purposive human actions to be so 'explained'. I shall now offer and discuss a slightly rephrased statement of the physicalist enterprise — one which is at first glance quite as unspecific as the first description, but which will prove more amenable to clarification. Physicalism, in this new version, is described as follows: it is the attempt to correlate explanations of actions couched in psychological terms with descriptions and explanations of cerebral states, events, and processes couched in neurophysiological terms. Now 'correlate' is quite as vague — if not more so — than 'explain', but this fact we shall use as an asset; at least it wears its vagueness on its face, which will be a constant reminder that we need to give it precise content. 'Reduce' would be considerably more specific, for we are familiar with what is involved in reducing one science to another; but in the next chapter I shall be arguing that physicalism does not aim for any reduction. Let us, then, remain temporarily content with 'correlate', taking it to stand for whatever relation it is that we eventually decide to hold between psychology and neurophysiology.

From this revised account of physicalism it is immediately evident that the project is one which involves two groups of scientists – this is the merest truism; the problem is an empirical problem engaging the attention of psychologists and neurophysiologists (who stand in, as before, for all the scientists studying the workings of the brain and central nervous system). In some way as yet unclarified these scientists are trying to ground psychology in neurophysiology; neurophysiology, in other words, we can regard as the more basic science. To say it is more basic is not to slight psychology, but rather to draw attention to two features of the proposed correlation: first, that neurophysiology is expected to give finer-grained and more detailed explanations on a micro-level of those phenomena which psychology describes and explains at a macro-level; second, that the micro-explanations of neurophysiology will be part and parcel of the more general endeavour of the physical sciences *in toto*, the endeavour to find a unitary model of explanation for all natural phenomena, animate and inanimate. In short, neurophysiology is regarded as more fundamental because it explains *why* the laws of psychology hold to the extent that they do, something that psychology itself cannot explain; and because it is believed to be reducible to the science we consider the most fundamental of all: physics.

Now whenever we are trying to work out a lawlike correlation, or indeed reduction, of two sciences, our aim is as follows: to take the observational statements, the laws, and the theoretical postulates that are discovered or asserted by one discipline and articulated in its vocabulary, and show how they may all be derived from or explained in terms of the laws of the other. More than this: we require the reducing, or more basic, science to explain as well why the laws of the reduced or less basic science hold to the extent they do; in other words, to explain *inter alia* where they cease to hold and why. Clearly, for such an enterprise to be successful, the observations, laws and regularities to be explained must be stated as precisely and unambiguously as possible. Unless they are so stated, we cannot discover if we have provided a complete correlation or not. The point is obvious: if one is trying to explain the claims, successes, and shortcomings of one empirical inquiry in terms of another, then we must have an unambiguous and precise formulation of just what those claims, successes, and shortcomings are. So if physicalism is to be shown either to hold or not to hold, it is just as important to formulate in an articulate and systematic way the body of knowledge and theory that comprises psychology as it is for neurophysiology.

One side of the relationship – the side of the physical sciences – promises to be adequate to meet this stringent demand for precise articulation. As we saw in chapter I, there seems no reason of principle why the physical sciences devoted to the study of the brain and central nervous system should not advance towards the goal of a clear, systematic, and internally consistent body of theory which may provide a comprehensive and detailed account of the functioning of the brain and body. Certainly such a goal is as yet far distant; but whatever one's criteria for a good theory may be, there seems no reason why these sciences should not eventually meet them.

We must demand the same high standards of psychology, the science that we hope to correlate with neurophysiology. It will simply be a waste of time trying to provide such a correlation unless psychology has some substantial content – unless, that is, its explanations of human behaviour are penetrating, comprehensive, fruitful, and clear; in short, interesting. Moreover, if it is to be correlated in a lawlike way with a systematic body of theory, then its theory, too, must be systematically organised. For example, its ontological commitments must be clear: we must know exactly what theoretical entities the science acknowledges, and to what ontological category (event, state, process, etc.) they belong. Each theoretical entity is partially defined by theoretical postulates (laws linking theoretical item with theoretical item) and correspondence rules (rules linking theoretical entities with the observational data); hence, if we are to understand the theoretical superstructure at all, these postulates and rules must be unambiguous and clear. A good theory is one which claims comprehensiveness; so this superstructure of theoretical entities and postulates must be adequate to explain the greatest possible range of human behaviour – as much as possible of whatever it is that the psychology of action takes as its subject matter. Evidently we must have precise descriptions of the events to be explained; these descriptions, too, will depend upon the nature and adequacy of the theoretical superstructure, since it is only by reference to the theory to be confirmed or refuted that one can say what *sorts* of observations of actions are relevant to this end. All this, and more besides, we require of psychology if ever the claim of physicalism – that this science can indeed be grounded in neurophysiology – is to be worth testing.

These prerequisites for a fruitful theory are, however, usually forgotten when philosophers are debating the viability of correlating mental with physical explanations. For it turns out – as we have seen in the previous chapter – that what we demand of physicalism is that neurophysiology should ground our familiar 'mental events': the belief that it is raining, a desire to stay dry, an intention to speak, the motive of revenge, the memory of Vienna. It is clear why we assume without hesitation that such phenomena are indeed the items to be correlated with neurophysiological items; when we explain the behaviour of ourselves and others, something we do daily and hourly, we do it in terms of these mental events – and we have a very rich stock of them. By citing beliefs, desires, emotions, moods, and the like, we can explain a huge range of diverse human activity; we can, too, frame rules of thumb and generalise about the way someone tends to behave, and so often make fairly reliable predictions. Our accounts of human behaviour in these terms can be penetrating and illuminating in the extreme, as countless novels bear witness. It is tempting to suppose that the subject matter and the vocabulary of psychology consist of a codified and systematised statement of our common-sense generalisations and observations, and hence of the entire rich ontology of all the mental events used in such explanatory endeavours; and that this is the subject matter and the vocabulary to be correlated with the physical sciences.

Such a supposition would be false; and seriously and significantly false. Our mental vocabulary is but one part of our ordinary language vocabulary, and the explanations framed in such terminology are likewise part of the common-sense description and explanation of the environment. But science is what begins just where common sense leaves off or proves inadequate. Let us go briefly into some of the more striking differences between science and common sense.

First, then, common-sense explanations tend naturally enough to be concerned with matters clearly relevant to human needs and preoccupations, and to stop there. Practical wisdom, by happy accident, discovered that fresh fruit could prevent scurvy (a bit of nautical know-how that led to the British being called 'Limeys'). It was not, however, concerned to discover any explanation for the efficacy of fruit. This lack of concern for an explanation can often lead to trouble. If one simply possesses the information that DDT-spraying kills pests on crops but does not know why or how, then there may be worse difficulties ahead when those pests evolve a strain immune to DDT, or when the plants themselves are seen to be damaged by too much spraying. When we know *why* some measure of this kind is effective, then we will know, too, what its limitations are, and in what conditions it is likely to be unsuccessful or indeed damaging; but this sort of knowledge is not the province of unaided common sense but requires the experimental methodology of the sciences. Practical wisdom in such matters can only suffice in a static, unchanging environment, and shows up its incompleteness when that alters a little. So we can conclude that science moves in to illuminate the relations between common-sense generalisations and the wider background of related facts and physical laws; it shows how and when the reliance on practical know-how should be limited, by explaining just why it works when it does.

Second, concerned as it is with matters of human interest and importance, practical wisdom naturally groups together phenomena that strike us as interestingly similar, and distinguishes those that are apparently different. But the immediately apparent similarities and differences may be irrelevant or misleading. Without zoology, we should undoubtedly still be classifying together Wolf (*Canis*) and the Tasmanian wolf; but however similar they appear, phylogenetically they are far apart. Conversely, without benefit of Newton, common sense could see nothing interesting or important to connect the orbits of the moon, the tide cycle, the paths of bullets and other projectiles, and the rise of liquids in narrow tubes – it took Newtonian mechanics to relate the kinds of motion of all these apparently dissimilar phenomena in a sophisticated scientific theory.

Third, common-sense explanations are debarred from penetrating explanatory power by the generality and imprecision of their scope. This renders them relatively immune from falsification but restricts their depth and informative content. Ordinary-language terms cannot usually provide the detailed precision that science demands; obviously not, for ordinary language has countless uses for its statements other than simple description, explanation, and prediction, which is all that science requires. Thus in everyday terminology we may call 'water' that which falls from the sky, that which comprises the Dead Sea, Loch Ness, and chlorinated swimming pools, distilled water, and even sweat. We know by practical wisdom that when chilled enough, water freezes. But this statement, and others like it, is virtually unfalsifiable and trivially true; it is not affected by the regular failure of most oceans to freeze even when puddles are freezing at the same temperature; nor does it take into account the effect of altitude or the chemical properties that various sorts of 'water' possess. For statements that have penetrating and detailed explanatory and predictive power we must turn to scientific research and scientific terminology: the quantification of degrees of temperature, chemical analyses, the effects of altitude — and thus we replace vagueness by specificity, untestability by informative falsifiability, and as a corollary can link our data about water and its freezing to a background body of theory, such as the study of H_2O molecules. Ordinary language needs the imprecision of a term like 'water' for its other roles: to warn one that one can drown in water (any water), and that any boiling water can scald; to express pleasure in the sound of a stream or the beauty of reflections in water. Given the multiplicity of uses to which we put ordinary language, the imprecision or lack of sharp definition of terms like 'water' is an indispensable asset not a handicap; but they cannot be used for the precise descriptive and explanatory purposes of a science.

One must add, of course, that science — any science — may borrow a term common in everyday idiom and employ it in a theory; this happens frequently. Physicists have taken over concepts such as 'force', 'mass', and 'energy'; experimental psychologists use the term 'memory' and 'information'; sociologists may talk of the needs or beliefs of groups. But whenever any such term is adopted, it must also be adapted: given a sharp definition that imposes on the term a precision it usually lacks in common idiom. 'Energy', for example, is defined exactly in terms of mass and velocity, and this distances it from the ordinary-language idea of energy as 'what we get when we eat Weetabix for breakfast'. Merely to employ terms found in common language is no indication of any lack of scientific exactness — the borrowed terms have suffered a sea-change because of the scientific demand for unambiguous clarity.

So scientific terms tend to be defined exactly, and this is because of the descriptive and explanatory roles that they must bear; but there is another reason why scientific statements can be rich in predictive and explanatory power, which provides the fourth difference from the statements of common sense. Science can explain in greater detail and depth than common sense because it employs highly abstract theoretical notions (e.g., neutrons, genes, drives, quarks, the superego, and the like) which enjoy a *prima facie* remoteness from the observable items and properties of common sense. Theoretical entities are deliberately postulated, and theoretical postulates are devised to link them, in an endeavour to get behind, beyond or beneath the recurring traits and qualities of observable phenomena; they show how surface regularities may be a function of, and hence explained by, pervasive relational and structural properties which are not observable, but which are found in many other observable items besides those under study. Thus events of a particular kind are explained in terms of a far wider background, by means of abstract and often abstruse concepts and laws which provide a more thoroughgoing account of them. This feature of scientific theories evidently explains the first two differences from common sense noted above: science can assess the adequacy of common-sense rules of thumb precisely because its theoretical structure can set them against a wider background; and it is this same structure which determines the classifications of observable phenomena, classifications that will often differ widely from those made by common sense.

Fifth – and this is a point especially relevant to the difference between common-sense 'psychologising' and the systematic science of psychology – the difference in *explananda*. Very largely, and I would say predominantly, our central interest and concern when endeavouring to understand other people lies with the specific action of an individual. Why did Flossie flounce out of the party only ten minutes after she arrived? Why did Jim, of all people, join the RAF? Why is he lying? Why have they broken off their engagement? Why did he play the second movement so much faster than he usually does? Generalisations about the behaviour of people in general (as distinct from the generalisations we may form about an individual's behaviour) are, in fact, rare in ordinary language; and when they do occur, tend to be trivial in content and proverbial in style: 'The family that prays together stays together', 'Once bitten, twice shy', 'You can't teach an old dog new tricks'. Our primary interest does not lie in discovering such generalisations. Survival in the social jungle requires the ability to understand and predict the actions of individuals – to explain unique bits of behaviour. But a science of psychology must put the emphasis quite elsewhere: in action types, not action tokens. (An analogous distinction might be drawn between the disciplines of history and sociology, unless one is convinced − wrongly, in my view − of the adequacy of the 'covering-law' model for historical research.)

The point is important, and merits further discussion and defence. An illustration from medicine will help. Suppose there are four people in the UK suffering from what appears to be the same disease − the symptoms in each case are the same − but the disease itself is unknown. The family GP is concerned to cure Bob (or Carol, Ted, or Alice), but this he will be unable to do, except by happy chance, unless the medical researcher has succeeded in his task, which is to identify the disease and its causes, and discover an antidote. Now the laboratory researcher will certainly need to know a great deal about Bob (and Carol, Ted and Alice) if he is to get anywhere; he would look, for example, to see if there are any common factors in their medical case-histories, or if they have all recently visited the same area of a certain country, or if they have all been handling the same kind of chemicals, or if they have all been treating sick donkeys − and so forth. Nevertheless he will be interested in Bob's case-history rather than in Bob. In other words, he seeks to find and isolate in the four individual case-histories the common factors which help him identify the causes and nature of the disease; and that it is Bob whose case-history he is in fact studying is entirely beside the point. His aim is to contribute to medical knowledge by explaining a hitherto mysterious illness, no matter who is the sufferer.

The psychologist parallels the researcher rather than the family GP. His concern is with behaviour of a certain type, no matter who is the agent, no matter when. Individual cases of a type of action are just that − individual cases; and he will be interested in the individual agents just to the extent that by comparing their activities he may be led to discover or postulate a common explanation, an explanation that will serve to account for any further instances of that action. This amounts to the truism that any science seeks to provide *general* laws about its subject matter; but it is a truism of which the implications are too often neglected in discussions of physicalism.

The defender of ordinary-language psychologising may here make a move comparable to one often made by covering-law theorists of historical research. The move is to argue that ordinary-language explanations of action, which typically take the form: 'A ϕed because he wanted W and believed that p', must appeal at least tacitly to a lawlike generalisation of the following sort: '*Ceteris paribus*, anyone who wants W and believes that p will ϕ.' The '*ceteris paribus*' clause must, of course, include stipulations that the ϕ-er is like A in the relevant respects (i.e., having relevantly similar aims, attitudes, addictions, ambitions, etc.), and that the circumstances are also relevantly similar. Such a move has considerable initial appeal. Certainly we do have intuitions about what most people would regard as rational if they were in A's position and had his want and his belief; to explain A's action is to appeal to some common understanding of this kind, by showing that it is what we would tend to expect of any person of that sort were he to be in the position in which A believes himself to be. Further, we can expect much light on human behaviour to be cast by serious attempts to spell out these backing generalisations; maybe those people whom we regard as the best and most understanding observers of human nature are precisely those who, tacitly or explicitly, have a grasp of such general hypotheses. Nevertheless, this kind of understanding will not be scientific. The generalisations involved may be modified without limit but can never attain the status of *laws*, even of statistical laws, as the *ceteris paribus* clauses cannot ever be delimited, even roughly. 'Too much happens to affect the mental that is not itself a systematic part of the mental';[1] only within a theory that is not only comprehensive but also closed, a theory that determines the range of variable factors, do we find genuine laws — laws capable of improvement right up to the theoretically possible goal of complete coherence with all the evidence, by drawing upon other concepts, laws, and postulates which help constitute the theory. Our mental vocabulary does not, and should not be expected to, constitute a closed theory; its 'laws' remain forever generalisations, barred from the title 'scientific' by the irremediable open-endedness of the *ceteris paribus* clauses — and indeed by the preceding four considerations listed above. In short, even if practical wisdom were to become as interested in formulating and defending generalisations about human behaviour as it is to explain individual human actions (and this is highly unlikely), such a change of emphasis would not transform it into a science.

The sixth difference is closely related to the fifth, again marking a difference between the *explananda* of science and common sense; but whereas the previous discussion concerned the type/token distinction, this concerns complexity. We should never expect scientists to predict the exact time a leaf leaves a tree in autumn, the precise route it takes through the air, and the exact time and place it touches the ground; and that we do not expect such information from scientists is not simply because we know the inadequate state of meteorology and biology. It is rather that in principle such events may be predictable, but only if one were to put together large numbers of facts and laws from a variety of diverse sciences — botany, biology, meteorology, physics. Each of the sciences in question, however, seeks first and foremost to explain common and fundamental traits of its own subject matter; applied science must await pure science. In exactly the same way the kind of psychology in which we are interested — that is, the psychology that is deliberately aiming at a correlation with neurophysiology – will not try to explain why Flossie flounced out of a party only ten minutes after she arrived. Such an event, if predictable at all, will require the putting together of many facts and laws of several branches of the psychological studies, including social psychology; and each of the individual sciences involved has, again, first and foremost its own subject matter of which it hopes to explain basic and fundamental traits. For our kind of psychology the overriding concern is with the most general, common, indispensable, and pervasive abilities of people – abilities that are required for each and every complex action, no matter what other, incidental, features may be involved. Thus it seeks to explain our ability to remember for short, medium, and long periods of time; our ability to recognise patterns; to solve problems of various related and unrelated kinds; to rank preferences; to classify; and so on and so forth. If we now put points five and six together, we shall not be surprised to find that the psychology in which we are interested has little if anything to say about the human actions that rouse our curiosity in everyday life; instead it will take sizeable groups of people into laboratories, set them to a task such as memorising lists of five-digit numbers, and study the results. For only by such means can it build up a comprehensive theory about the most basic and pervasive characteristics of each and every human action.

All six points cited above make the following conclusion quite inescapable: ordinary-language descriptions and explanations of action have nothing to do with the project of physicalism. Common sense could never provide the body of knowledge of the required sort – nothing that could be correlated with neurophysiological findings. We have seen that it lacks the theoretical superstructure which enables us to get beyond a surface level of explanation; the conceptual framework of the mental cannot be moulded into a comprehensive closed theory; the concern of everyday explanation is not with fundamental general traits but with specific complex actions. Undoubtedly the most significant and central hindrance to ordinary language providing a science of human action is the nature of the mental vocabulary; which, like other ordinary-language terms, is wholly unfitted for scientific purposes (cf. point three above, and the remarks at the end of the last chapter). Countless tasks other than those of description and explanation are required of it; e.g., to warn: 'He thinks you're hostile to him'; to suggest or imply: 'She's certainly very *clever*'; to blame: 'You wanted him to fail'; to exhort: 'You can try to do it'; to reproach: 'He trusted you'; to congratulate: 'Your decision saved us from disaster'; to threaten: 'You're beginning to try my patience'; to assess: 'She's too emotional for such a task'; to condemn: 'He's guilty of the crime'; and many more. Further, shades of implications which are quite independent of description and explanation help determine our choice of terms even when we are ostensibly describing; to say 'He believes that p' may, in context, carry vastly different overtones from 'He remembers that p', 'He thinks that p', 'He knows that p', 'He's sure that p', 'He feels that p', 'His opinion is that p', 'He holds that p'. We make exceedingly fine linguistic discriminations with beautiful precision; but these discriminations are not in the interests of more precise *description* – we do not feel the need to distinguish four different kinds of memory, for example.[2]

This rich and flexible array of terms with overlapping and interlocking uses makes it quite impossible to say what constitutes the mental ontology. Indeed I would go further and contend that there is no 'mental ontology' at all, nor should we look for one. Contrast science: any science strives to put beyond all doubt what is meant by, say, postulating the existence of an electron (a particle), or talking of the instantaneous velocity of a point-mass (the limit of an infinite series of ratios); and the ranges of scientific terms are not blurred – instantaneous velocity is sharply distinguished from instantaneous acceleration. In short, categorial status is apparent, ranges of terms demarcated. But our mental vocabulary freely reifies – or gives the appearance of reifying – 'beliefs', 'memories', 'thoughts', 'intentions', 'plans', 'motives', 'desires', 'emotions', 'wishes', 'wants', etc.; but also it reifies *acts* of thinking, remembering, hoping, wishing, or wanting. A thought may be treated as an event, a disposition, a process, an occurrence; it may or may not be, also or instead, a memory, a belief, a prejudice, a guess, an opinion, a conviction, or something else. To repeat a metaphor used earlier, we can legitimately and irreproachably divide up the mental flux just as is most convenient for our purposes: reproaches are incurred only if we get puzzled because we are confounding the products of two different methods of slicing as though there were just one (we cannot, by *one* kind of division, end up with both 'mental images' and 'acts of visualising', any more than we can slice football into both 'kicks' and 'kickings'). One result of the later work of Wittgenstein has been to free us of two temptations; the first is to think that the mental flux comes ready sliced, that there really is an objective mental ontology, the second is to confuse the results of different ways of slicing, thereby generating philosophical problems.

A quotation from Feigl will sum up and conclude the argument of this chapter so far:[3]

The ordinary language approach, though often phenomenologically perceptive, is fraught with the dangers of a regression to the sort of commonsense psychology which is contained in the intuitive psychological understanding' that any person of some experience possesses anyway. This is the 'psychology' used quite effectively in the practical affairs of diplomats, ministers, politicians, businessmen, parents, nursemaids, and fishwives. There are few surprises, and hardly anything that could be incorporated in, for example, the theory of motivation.

So it is scientific psychology that is the other partner in the correlation with neurophysiology. This finding limits the role of the philosopher, *qua* philosopher of mind, considerably; for as with the physical sciences, so with psychological theory: its nature and content and the conceptual framework in which it is couched will be the business of the practising psychologist and not the philosopher. The philosopher of science may look into the structure of psychological theory, however; and it is indeed to the philosophy of psychology that we turn in the next chapter. But before we embark on that, there are some wholly general points about psychological theory that may profitably be mentioned here, since they either arise from, or are closely connected with, the themes we have been discussing.

The most vital general remark: it is clear from the arguments of chapter 2 that whatever the detailed content of the conceptual apparatus employed by a psychological theory may prove to be, we must find there some intensional terms; otherwise the description and the explanation of action are alike impossible. The briefest glance at the psychological literature suffices to show that contemporary psychology acknowledges this requirement – 'memory', for example, is intensional, as is a most common and pivotal notion in most current psychological theories, the notion of information. Many more intensional, or latently intensional, concepts will readily be found. So it may seem that in the present chapter we have come a long way to no purpose; all we have done is to replace intensional mental terms by intensional psychological terms, and the problem posed by intensionality looms as large as ever. It must somehow be solved.

The third general remark about psychological theory concerns neurophysiology too. I have argued that the kind of psychology in which we are interested is the kind that takes for granted the assumption that physicalism is in fact true – the kind that is deliberately working towards the desired correlation with neurophysiology. To test physicalism is precisely to study the viability of this enterprise. Given such an ambition, one obvious consequence is that the psychological theory must not postulate entities or processes which there are good grounds for believing to be incapable of neurophysiological realisation. To posit something like an information-retrieval mechanism in psychological theory is legitimate only if it is thought to be possible that some, perhaps enormously complicated, cerebroceptive structure or process may be correlated with it; on the other hand, a suggestion that something like an immaterial *élan vital* has causal efficacy in the brain would be scientifically barren – for neurophysiology could not produce a physical realisation of a non-physical process, nor would it know how to set about describing causal interactions between immaterial and material events. So, since we have the *truth* of physicalism as an indispensable working assumption, an important test of any psychological theory is that it does not debar itself from forming correlations with neurophysiology. One that fails to meet this requirement we shall call, quite simply, wrong.

There is another side to this interaction of psychology and neurophysiology: the fruits of psychological theory-construction may often be needed by neurophysiologists as they come to decide upon their own theoretical and ontological commitments. For consider that neurophysiologists are confronted with a ceaseless flux of neural activity in the brain;

there are about 10,000 million neurons, most in constant activation. Thus the behaviour of neurons will admit of a huge diversity of possible descriptions. Neural processes could be classified on the basis of the amount of electrical discharge, the extent or location of the brain tissue involved, the pattern properties of neural excitation, or by yet other criteria. Some suggested guidelines, however tentative, must be found to provide a principle of classification for cerebral events; and since neurophysiology is striving for a successful correlation with psychology, the optimum principle of classification will be one which helps to explain how the brain is organised to bring about overt behaviour. It is one function of psychology, as it studies the human agent at its macro-level of description, to suggest guidelines to enable neurophysiologists to classify relevantly at their micro-level. In short, neurophysiology without psychology would be blind.

The last general point about psychology again concerns its relationship with ordinary language. I have argued that the ontology, terms, and explanations of common sense have nothing to do with physicalism; and emphasis has shifted away from common sense, towards a scientific psychology. This may leave one with a residual unease; given that it is psychology that is to be correlated with neurophysiology, what then *are* we to say about the terms and the explanations of ordinary language? For example, what links or connections, if any, does our term 'belief' have with the psychological term 'information'? It seems unsatisfactory just to drop ordinary language entirely, for we believe that psychology and common sense must have something to do with one another.

There are two things that might be said in response to this perplexity, which is genuine enough. First, common sense has indeed been studying human behaviour through many centuries, and has amassed many detailed and informative observations about kinds of behaviour; we have a store of generalisations which, even if they do not amount to strictly scientific laws, are important, well-grounded, and interesting. Such findings cannot be ignored, and it is legitimate to require our psychology to take these insights and discoveries as *explananda*, and to account for them. Science should not be confused with common sense, but it is continuous with it; so whenever common sense has produced factual and interesting statements about human behaviour, these must become part of the subject matter of psychology, a part it can reasonably be challenged to explain. In this respect psychology is unlike a science such as biochemistry: we all have to engage, willy-nilly, in some common-sense 'psychology' in the interests of a social existence of any sort, as we do not have to engage in rudimentary biochemistry. So biochemists do not have a body of biochemical common sense to explain; but there is a fund of practical psychology with which psychologists must come to terms – we may postpone, but should not forget, our demand for a deeper understanding of our pre-scientific insights.

The second response to the problem does not mitigate it, but rather generalises it by casting it in a wider context. If the relation of everyday 'psychology' to psychology proper is problematic, it is nevertheless no *more* puzzling than is the relation between ordinary-language talk of chairs and tables and the physicists' talk of molecules, protons, and neutrons.[4] Psychology bears the same relation to ordinary language as does physics; this relation I certainly find difficult, although I have no good reasons for my dissatisfaction. The problem cannot be discussed at any length here; my suspicion is that there is a case for a 'peaceful co-existence' of everyday and scientific terminology, were we to give a cool and thorough Austinian analysis of, for example, the 'really' in such sentences as, 'Tables are really only collections of molecules' or,

'Remembering is really the retrieval of stored information-"bits".' What seems to me to be clear is that we should not see science as being in conflict with common sense – few physicists would assert that there are no such things as tables, and few psychologists that there are no such things as memories. Only extreme ontological absolutists would wish to hold such a position; they would indeed find no problem in the relation between science and common sense, for they would simply insist that we must supplant the latter by the former. But if in a more liberal vein we concede the integrity of each form of discourse, the problem stands; there is some comfort in the reflection that although we may be no closer to discovering the nature of reality, we have at least shown ourselves better aware of the complexities of the term 'reality'.

Notes

1 D. Davidson, 'Mental Events', in L. Foster and J.W. Swanson (eds), *Experience and Theory* (Massachusetts, 1970), p. 99.
2 As John Morton would like to do; see his 'A Functional Model for Memory', in D.A. Norman (ed.), *Models for Human Memory* (New York, 1970).
3 H. Feigl, *The 'Mental' and the 'Physical': The Essay and a Postscript* (Minnesota, 1967), p. 159.
4 Perhaps it is in one sense more puzzling in that chairs, tables, ships, and sealing wax are all indisputedly accepted individual items of our common-sense ontology, whereas as we have seen there is no comparable fixed ontology for our common-sense mental discourse. But this feature does not affect the main issue; it shows only that talk about the mental is more complex than talk about public, material objects.

CHAPTER 4

PSYCHOLOGY AND PRACTICE

I N the last chapter the emphasis shifted from the mental to the psychological; but the primary problem of intensionality seems not to have been shifted at all. On the contrary, the difficulty may appear to loom even larger; for one advantage of the intensional terms of our mental vocabulary is that they are at least familiar, whereas those of psychological theory we may expect to find unfamiliar and abstract. But despite appearances we have in fact reached a basis for no less than two solutions to the problem. The first will emerge from a consideration of scientific method in general, which shows how the intensionality of psychological terms is neatly neutralised by the demands of scientific practice; the second must await a description and discussion of one specific type of psychological methodology, for it depends upon one's willingness to adopt this kind of theory.

To begin with the first solution. The classical trouble with intensional sentences is, as we have seen, that they do not conform to the extensional logic of the physical sciences. The problem would disappear if, in a sentence of the form 'X ϕ s that p', where 'ϕ' is an intensional verb, we could substitute equivalences for equivalences within p; in other words, if we could legitimately treat intensional contexts extensionally. This is not so difficult as it may sound, so long as we thoroughly understand the aims and procedures of a science.

Example will supply the best explanation. I take a type of experiment that has been popular for fifty years, in which a number of subjects are asked to solve a problem of induction. They are given about thirty figures, each of which is labelled with a nonsense-syllable name. Some of the figures are labelled with the same name, and the subjects of the experiment are told that all the figures paired with the same name have something in common. They are expected to discover this common feature — i.e., to identify the class of figures falling under one name. The tests for success are of two kinds; one, they have to pick out from a set of *un*labelled figures those that belong with the named group; second, they are asked to describe verbally the feature criterial to the class. For instance, Hull paired nonsense-syllable names with tangles of lines, and the common feature of the figures labelled with a single name was the presence, somewhere in the tangles, of a Chinese character — upright, upside-down, or sideways on.[1] Smoke gave his subjects geometrical designs to examine;[2] Fisher used irregular shapes, and his distinguishing feature was a tangled, irregular pattern.[3] There are many other experiments of this type.[4]

A result common to all these experiments was that the subjects, after studying the labelled figures for a set time, were usually able to go on faultlessly to identify further (unlabelled) members of the class, although they generally failed to define the criterial feature. Of course, sometimes this feature defied verbal description — as in the case of Fisher's experiment — but even when it did not, the result was much the same. There could be complete success in picking out further members of the class combined with failure to indicate successfully what it was they all had in common. Moreover, when there were attempts to describe the common feature, these might be partially correct only; subjects might say the distinguishing feature was 'a triangle', whereas it was in fact an isosceles triangle – this although they had no hesitation in ruling out from the class those figures containing a triangle that was *not* isosceles. It would seem then that the belief 'a triangle is the distinguishing feature' could not serve to explain their successful selections. Descriptions of the distinguishing feature varied: the isosceles triangle might be described as 'an isosceles triangle', 'a triangle', 'a sandwich shape', and the like: but this diversity and imprecision were significantly independent of the success or failure of the subjects in their other task, that of picking out unlabelled members of the class.

Let us suppose an imaginary experiment of this type where the distinguishing feature is indeed an isosceles triangle, and five subjects have succeeded in the task of identifying unlabelled members of the class. When asked to describe the feature, A replies that it is an isosceles triangle. B thinks it is 'a sort of triangle', C just says it is a triangle, D that it is a sandwich shape, and E has nothing to offer. Suppose further that the psychologist is aiming here to provide an explanation for all five tokens of the one action type, the successful identification of members of a class. He has, in fact, a single *explanandum*; and we expect a single explanation, an explanation which will be adequate to account for each of the five instances of the behaviour in question. Evidently such an explanation must somehow express the fact that (as we would say in everyday terminology) they all in some sense know or have guessed what the criterial feature is. Further, the explanation must suffice to explain the same success in the same experiment when performed by F, G, H, I, and J on the preceding or following days. So we cannot be interested in any explanation that is peculiar to one of our five subjects.

One *false* description of the information possessed by any successful subject would be:

(1)   The sandwich shape is the distinguishing feature

False, because sandwiches come in many shapes and sizes; A and B may standardly eat oblong ones. Equally false would be C's offering:

(2)   A triangular shape is the distinguishing feature

This is false because not any triangular shape will do: it must be isosceles. But a true description of the information that they all possess would run:

(3)   The isosceles-triangle shape is the distinguishing feature

– *or any extensionally equivalent substitution thereof*.[5] For (3), or any standard logical equivalence, explains the behaviour of all the successful subjects; it is precisely the information that an unsuccessful participant in the experiment would lack.

In other words, quite apart from asking the subjects to *describe* the criterial feature, the psychologist is licensed (since he has to explain the regular successful performance of an action type) to *ascribe* to them just that information which is necessary, in this restricted experimental context, to account for their success. Whatever else is true of the subjects this at least must be: that they all possess the information expressed by (3); and that they all possess the information expressed by any sentence equivalent to (3).

A word is needed on this notion of 'information'. It would be erroneous to suppose that this concept, so widely used by psychologists in studying problem-solving behaviour, is our everyday concept. We tend to regard the possession of information as a matter of having the ability to tell, a linguistic matter; but psychologists employ the notions of acquiring and storing information in connection with non-human subjects as well as humans, and it does not usually make good sense to suppose that animals or birds hold propositional attitudes. Just as physicists adopt and adapt everyday terms like 'force', 'mass', and 'energy', so 'information' is taken over and defined for use in psychological theory, and becomes a theoretical notion. It thus no longer denotes some introspectible datum or state to which the subjects should be expected to *testify*. Like all theoretical notions, its meaning is given partly by the theoretical postulates that describe its relations to other such theoretical entities and processes as input analysis, information-storage and retrieval mechanisms; these postulates comprise the theoretical superstructure of the science, showing the use, and hence part of the meaning of, the related theoretical items. The rest of the meaning of the theoretical term is given by the correspondence rules, which describe the kind of relation the theoretical entity bears to observable behaviour, a relation illustrated by our example. We are not dealing, then, with the everyday notion of 'information'; but the fact that it has been borrowed from ordinary language provides the imagination with some grasp on what is essentially a highly abstract concept. The psychological use of the term 'information' differs most significantly from the everyday concept in that it presupposes no answers to the questions of (a) how any subject happens to conceptualise this information at some time t; and (b) whether he does so at all. For when we are trying to explain an action such as the successful discrimination of members of a class, then the particular stream of consciousness, or inner verbal commentary, of the actors (if indeed there is such a stream or commentary) is not an *explanandum* itself, nor need it be part of the *explanans*. Although we could, of course, attempt to explain the activity of the production of linguistic tokens, it is essential to realise that such a project would be an entirely different enterprise from the attempt to explain shape-selection.

If we think of 'information', then, as a technical and theoretical psychological term, we can specify the correct description of the information that must be attributed to any successful participant in the experiment – much as a medical researcher discovers a virus that must be supposed common to all sufferers from influenza of strain S – and that description is correct which is such that (a) if non-equivalent descriptions were substituted, they would fail to explain some of the successful results, and (b) if dictionary-derived equivalences were substituted, they would leave the successful explanation unaffected. 'Information' is an intensional term, and is the psychologist's closest analogue to our 'belief', but it is treated purely extensionally. The propriety of extensional treatment is assured by the fact that scientific method aims at the explanation of action types, and not of A's action ϕ at time t; so the proffered explanation must be such that any performance of ϕ in the same condition is accounted for. Where we find differences in behaviour, *there* we have to look for corresponding differences in the explanations cited; but where the behaviour is the same, as it is in our hypothetical experiment, we need a single explanation. And part of the explanation that is needed to explain the successful performances of A, B, C, D, and E is given by describing the information they all alike possess.[6]

This, then, is a beginning. We now have a way of talking legitimately of 'the same information' being possessed by several people, as we did not have for talking of 'the same belief'. We move on next to see how these 'harmlessly' intensional descriptions of psychological theory may be correlated with the purely extensional statements of neurophysiology. There is a specific kind of psychological and neurophysiological method which can so correlate them; this is the method of functionalism, sometimes called structural-functional analysis. I shall first describe the method briefly, and then add a few explanatory comments.

A. Outline of a Method

The *analysandum* of a functional analysis is some system S (e.g. a society, an income-group, an individual, a record player, one hemisphere of the brain). All that is required of any system S is that it should be possible (whether profitable or not is another matter) to view it as consisting of systematically organised parts – an extremely undemanding requirement. Next, each chosen S must be defined, or given an unequivocal 'boundary', in terms of its state G of proper, characteristic, or efficient functioning. Examples of such G-states could be: stability in a society, health in an organism, the behavioural repertoire of a human agent, reliable sound-production in a record player. G will usually be more informatively treated as consisting of a set of states $g_1, g_2, \ldots, g_n$, which collectively spell out what it is for the chosen S to be in its state G of normal functioning; for example, 'reliable sound-production' can be broken down into items including 'good bass control' (g_m), 'with a smoothly revolving turntable' (g_n), for the S which is a record player; and 'health' could be specified in greater detail by citing 'having a body temperature of 98.4°' (g_o), 'having efficient metabolic and circulatory processes' (g_p), for the S which is a human organism. A list of such g's is in effect part of a definition of the chosen S: the description of the characteristic states and behavioural repertoire tells us precisely under what description (e.g. human agent or human organism) the S is to be identified.

Third, we need a set R $(r_1, r_2, \ldots, r_m)$ of functional prerequisites for the set G; R is the set of conditions necessary for a system S to remain in its state G. Typically, R consists of processes which we discover or postulate to explain each g. For example, we discover that the pumping of the heart (r_1) is required *inter alia* for the g described as 'having good blood circulation'; in sociology we find cited highly abstract and postulated functional requirements such as 'pattern maintenance', 'interest articulation', or 'tension management', to take three at random.[7]

Fourth, and finally, the framework of functionalism demands a set of structural items X (x_1, x_2, ..., x_r) which actually perform the functions that are members of R. The heart, x_m, pumps blood, r_a; Parliament, x_n, fulfils a variety of functions in a society; the spindle of a record player, x_o, helps fulfil the function of turning the turntable.

B. *Commentary on the Outline*

(1)   The preceding outline describes functionalism wherever it occurs — in economics, social anthropology, political theory, mechanics, etc. Sitting so loosely upon its putative subject matter, it cannot yet be a candidate for critical assessment or evaluation, for *qua* framework it says nothing about what sorts of items would typically go into the S, G, R, or X sets, says nothing about the kind of research it facilitates and fosters — in fact it has as yet made no claims to be assessed. Critical evaluation can begin only after it has been carefully and exactly applied to a given domain, and for a specific research project. The method may be wholly unsuited to many kinds of investigation.

(2)   We have a bewildering array of choices when we are choosing an S for psychology. Consider how variously man can be described. His nature may be thought divine — God is in him (or *vice versa*). He is a being guided by instinct or by self-interest, by a drive towards self-realisation, status, or reward; by a drive to maximise stimulation or perhaps to minimise it by a search for peace. He is the dash between S and R in stimulus-

response behaviourism; he is a converter of food energy, sexual energy, or libido; he is a utilities-maximising games-player; perhaps he is best seen as an advanced rat, monkey, or pattern-recognising computer; perhaps he is *sui generis*. Many of these descriptions offer viable objects of psychological study. However, the tendency of physiological psychology (unlike, say, ego-psychology or personality theory, which have as yet no direct stake in the defence of physicalism) has been to regard the individual as an agent of purposive, problem-solving behaviour;[8] even this admits of a variety of different specifications of the S at issue. Let us call the man-as-problem-solver S^*. Then, as sub-classes of S^* we may find: man-as-pattern-recogniser (S^*_p), man-as-chess-player (S^*_c); or, moving from specific kinds of problem to consider aspects of problem-solving behaviour in general, we might find man-as-ranker-of-preferences (S^*_r). All these, and there will be many more, offer psychologists legitimate *analysanda* as they examine S^*. Ultimately, it is clear, the sub-classes of S^* must be integrated into the wider analysis of S^* (just as, ideally, S^* should one day be merged with the functional analyses of personality theorists, ego-psychologists, and social psychologists). S^* itself can be examined only indirectly, through its various constitutive S's. For, obviously enough, we must always have exhaustively specified *kinds* of problems if we are to secure detailed and informative data.

(3)   Since the S for functional analysis in psychology is so open to diverse description, offering *analysanda* that may be sketched in more or less detail or comprehensiveness, the set G will be correspondingly variable too – since, as we have seen, it is in terms of G that we distinguish one S from another. Now it will be essential to aim for a constant level of descriptive generality in the delineation of any set G. This, as we have already noted, seems by no means easy. Actions are open to

description at various levels; we can specify them more or less generally, or in ways that absorb more or less of what may in other descriptions count as consequences or circumstances. The question 'What did he do?' has, out of context, no privileged single answer. But we are required by functional analysis to fix upon a constant level of abstractness in the description of whatever behaviour we are at that time concerned to analyse; without such constancy we could not decide what it is for two individuals to be exhibiting the *same* behaviour g_1, and what it is for them to be exhibiting different behaviours g_2 and g_3. Example: Smith puts out his right hand to signal a right turn; Jones flips the indicator switch; and Robinson puts out his right hand to see if it is raining. If we decide that Smith and Jones are doing the same thing, and Robinson something different, the g-descriptions must make this clear; for then we should look to find the same r's to explain Smith's and Jones's behaviour, and different r's to explain Robinson's. An over-general level of behaviour description could make a cat and a mousetrap 'exhibit the same behaviour' (a neat example supplied by Kalke[9]); conversely, too detailed a description would make practically every action unique. Nevertheless the problem for functional analysis is not as grave as it is for any ordinary-language 'psychological theory'. In our switch from the everyday descriptions of action, which take unique and highly complex performances as their subject matter, to scientific descriptions which study simple but pervasive types of behaviour, we can expect to find much more agreement about the clearest and most profitable level of description. If one is setting subjects a defined problem, in controlled laboratory conditions with a restricted choice of appropriate action, there cannot be much latitude left for diversity of description. Common sense and trial and error will be our guidelines here, and they will not be overburdened.

Moreover, the framework of functionalism provides scope for – even demands – both general and detailed levels of action description. The members of a given set G may be structured hierarchically, with a broadly characterised g, for example 'catching mice', broken down into its constitutive action elements: 'waiting' (g_a), 'slinking' (g_b), 'pouncing' (g_c), and 'biting' (g_d). Analogously, a chess player who has mastered the Sicilian Defence must be credited with mastery of the combinations of specific moves that constitute the ploy; and any of these constitutive g's may itself require dissection into yet more minute g-elements. The lowest-level (most detailed and specific) descriptions of g's – those at the bottom of the hierarchy – will be pragmatically fixed as those descriptions by means of which two individuals may sensibly be assessed to see if they are, or are not, doing the same thing in similar circumstances; and this pragmatic choice will differ from experiment to experiment, and will depend upon the purposes of the investigation.

(4)   Just as we cannot fix the S under analysis without filling in the set G, so G in its turn requires examination of the set R before we can list its constituents. Indeed, it would be a mistake to draw any hard and fast line between the G and R sets; an imaginary functional analysis of the simple washing machine will show this clearly. Suppose that this system, S_m, is given a set G consisting of a single member, 'washing clothes', g_m. Then the members of R required to explain how S_m performs g_m might include, as r_1, ..., r_5, 'soaking', 'soaping', 'agitating', 'rinsing', and 'drying'. But evidently these five r's could equally legitimately be included in the set G, the set of capacities comprising the characteristic behavioural repertoire of S_m; for patently a washing machine does soak, soap, agitate, rinse, and dry clothes. If these capacities were to be included in G, then altogether different members of R must be sought to

explain how S_m manages to perform them. Indeed if, as I shall be arguing shortly, members of R must, like G-members, be formed into hierarchies, we should envisage the G-R sets as forming an unbroken continuum.[10] We may draw the dividing line between them at various points − not arbitrarily, but for sound purpose-relative considerations − and it will always be movable. This point should not surprise us. The set R is cited to explain G; and we have already seen that description and explanation cannot be sharply distinguished. What counts as a description in one context provides an explanation in another. Possibly, functional analysis in psychology will tend to regard the human agent as a system with an observable G, and consign the unobservables, the posited or hypothesised internal processes, to R; but in any domain, and particularly in psychology, what counts as observable or not is highly problematical. Nevertheless, let us assume for convenience that G does consist of observable instances of problem-solving behaviour, and R of the internal and hypothesised theoretical functions cited to explain it.

Clearly the kind of r listed will vary according to the detail of the relevant g-description. If a g for a record player were described as 'turntable revolving at 16, 33, 45, or 78 rpm', we would need more detailed r's to explain that than if it were simply described as 'revolving turntable'. That point is sufficiently obvious. Equally so is the comment that a *set* of r's (conjoined, disjoined, in disjunctive conjunctions or conjunctive disjunctions) may be required to explain a single g. Actions can and do have complex determinants. On the other hand the same r's may enter into the explanation of different g's. The moral of this is that it would be foolish to expect a one-to-one correlation between G and R members; this will hold true of any functional analysis.

(5)   As R is to G, so is X to R. Just as a given g, for example

'mastery of the Sicilian Defence', may need to be broken down into constituent, subordinate g's before we seek r's to explain it, so likewise any postulated r may require dissection into smaller contributory functions, more detailed and specific r's, which combine to secure the original r. In other words, there is no guarantee that for any particular r there will be a unique x, or set of x's, to fulfil it *as described*. It may need to be broken down into component functions, some of which in their turn may require further dissection, before structurally isolable x's can be found, singly or in combination, to meet the postulated r's. For example, if among the r's for a washing machine we had 'maintaining an adequate water supply' (r_1), it would be useless to look for the part of the machine that is 'a water supplier'. Nor is there a set of items, $x_1, ..., x_n$, which all do a bit of water-supplying. There are of course structural items which are ultimately responsible for maintaining an adequate water supply; but they do this not by collectively 'supplying water' but by performing such functions as 'regulating inflow' (r_a), 'shutting off supply' (r_b), 'checking water level' (r_c), and so on. It is r_a, r_b and r_c which realise r_1; and only indirectly, by fulfilling r_a, r_b and r_c, do the relevant x's secure r_1. Descending orders of subordinate r's may ramify for some time before meeting their structural realisations. Much here will depend upon what structural items the ontology of the theory acknowledges; some x's may fulfil relatively general functions, others only more detailed ones.

Because of the practical difficulties inherent in the study of the living brain, the theories actually put forward by experimental psychologists to account for some bit of behaviour g_k may be competent only to postulate the requisite r's at a fairly molar level. These psychologists may not know whether neurophysiological research has come up with brain masses or cerebral processes that are both morphologically identifiable and also competent to perform the functions, the r's, which the experimental psychologists have postulated. The psychologist who observes human beings only from the outside is restricted to indicating the basic r's which, as he believes, there must be brain structures to meet; how they are to be met, directly or indirectly, is the neurophysiologists' problem. It is, after all, most unlikely that there is a handily convenient set of neural structures ready to fulfil, singly or conjointly, r's such as 'information-storing (retrieving, processing)', or 'analysing input' as described. Certainly if the r's that psychologists postulate cannot be met even indirectly by any type of brain item, this is proof positive that the hypothesised r's are the wrong ones; but their hypotheses are not refuted by a failure to find x's that meet the r's directly.

(6)   There is no absolute logical distinction that can be driven between r's and x's, functions and structures. For first, neurophysiologists may have reason to suspect the existence of a functionally relevant brain item of some sort, and yet not be in a position to locate and identify it physically; in which case that item may be 'known' only by virtue of the function it performs. The gene was so introduced originally: it was 'the item which did such-and-such', and was independently identified later. Second, the items taken to be the basic or most fundamental elements of the brain may not be explicitly 'structural' or material things (as neurons are), but may rather be items such as electrical charges or pattern configurations. Third, what neurophysiologists call 'basic' depends upon the current state of science (as of course it does in all sciences); and so items may be assigned to the r or x categories in virtue of the role they happen to be playing in a particular functional analysis – which role may vary from one scientist, or time, to another scientist, or time. In short, there is no sharp distinction worth drawing between function and structure; what

pragmatic distinction may be employed at any time depends on how the relevant brain item is described, and *this* depends upon the current state of neurophysiological research.[11]

(7)   A more obvious point. Any given x, or set of x's, may singly or in combination fulfil several r's in one or more functional analyses, just as some of the same r's maẙ be cited to help explain diverse g's. In other words, one would hope and expect that the same (or at least largely overlapping) sets of r's and x's could be used to explain, for example, both draughts-playing and chess-playing. This we hope because it is one important aim of psychophysiology to discover the most economical set of r's and x's capable of explaining a range of tasks; there is evident need for such economy, for some of the r's and x's in question will be the theoretical entities or processes of psychology and neurophysiology, and considerations of simplicity in theory-construction demand that we attempt to restrict their number. Ability to account for the observable data (the g's) must, of course, usually override the pull towards simplicity; but the pull should not be under-emphasised. It is the attempt to explain as much as possible in terms of as little as possible that brings out the concealed similarities and dissimilarities in the functioning of the brain when the agent is confronted with tasks of apparently diverse sorts; and only by striving after theoretical economy can we eventually discover fundamental and pervasive features of brain operation.

(8)   Some r's may be met by observable brain structures even when the analysis is yet at a macro-level. For there are, after all, many readily isolable brain masses such as the temporal lobe, the cortex, the diencephalon, the two hemispheres, Broca's area and Wernicke's area; such large brain masses may fulfil complex and generally described functions – for example, one can say that the left hemisphere is

responsible for the faculty of speech in most right-handed people. Now these items, which in a particular functional analysis may be included in the X set, are in turn highly complex and structured systems themselves. The practical consequence of this observation is, of course, that there is room to initiate another functional analysis, where the original x – Wernicke's area, for example, a brain mass that is certainly cited in functional explanations of aphasia and related brain injuries[12] – becomes the S for a new research project, and its *soi-disant r* or r's are transformed into a g or g's, i.e. into capacities of Wernicke's area that are now to be subjected to explanation. Indeed, until we reach base level – and remember that this means only 'until we reach what scientists are currently calling the "base level"' – there will be a descending series of functional analyses nestling into one another like Chinese boxes, breaking down the complex structures of the brain into smaller and more specialised functions and structures. Eventually we may reach a neuron, or a neural circuit, which has but one highly specialised function, that of 'discharging'. Above that we have an ascending and interlocked series of cerebral complexes, each of which may prove to be an x or an S, depending upon what functional analysis we are considering. (I allow, of course, that much detailed research in neurophysiology can and must be done independently of functionalism: I am not suggesting that every stage of every research activity must be directed towards a particular functional analysis. My point is rather that the interrelation of psychology and neurophysiology should be seen in terms of functionalism; either science may use other methodologies as well.)

So much for the discussion of the method. We can now suggest the second solution to the problem of intensionality – a 'solution' which rather dissolves than solves the problem. Let us agree that the psychologist, trying to build a theory of action but restricted to a molar level of description, will have to specify the behavioural repertoire G, and the functional prerequisites R cited to account for G, in sentences laden with intensionality. He may talk, for example, of the processing, storing, and retrieving of information; or of certain brain mechanisms analysing input, or sending signals to other structures. Such descriptions, he will claim, are literally true.[13] Thus we have several functions, or r's, which are described intensionally; but, as part of the macro-level theory of the experimental psychologist, they will be functions high up in the hierarchy of r's. As we know, there are two possibilities at the next stage of the functional analysis; the first, if no structural item or items can be found to fulfil those functions as described. In this case, the functions in question have to be dissected into their component functions – we have to find more detailed and specialised r's which combine to realise the original, more generally described, r's. However, the more specific the function, the less the likelihood of intensionality – for at the micro-level, if we reach the x's which are neurons, and their r, which is 'firing', we find no intensionality at all. The second possibility is that some complex brain mass *is* competent to perform the generally described functions, without the need to break down those functions into smaller component bits. But whenever this occurs the brain mass itself will be a complex structured system, in its turn subject to a functional analysis – and again we set off in search of more detailed functions to explain its behavioural repertoire. The result in either case is that the greater the detail of the research, the more inflexible will be the functions that are performed by micro-structures or micro-processes of the brain; intensional descriptions are needed only when functions are complex and flexible.

Intensionality, instead of being an obstacle, becomes an indispensable aid to the macro-level of what now proves to be a single science — which we may as well call psychophysiology.

There are, then, two attractive consequences of embracing the functionalist methodology. The first is that we do not have to reduce psychology to neurophysiology in order to defend the viability of physicalism; we unite the two into one science, affirming their complementarity and mutual interdependence in a spiral of research of which the outermost circles are what we used to call psychology, the innermost, neurophysiology. The second consequence is that intensionality rides only on the outer circles, loosening its grip upon the conceptual apparatus precisely as it becomes no longer necessary. Where and when it vanishes altogether is not at all important; it has vanished by the end, as the completed functional analysis will show.

Notes

1 C.L. Hull, 'Quantitative Aspects of the Evolution of Concepts', *Psychological Monographs* 28 (1920), no. 1 (whole no. 123).

2 K.L. Smoke, 'An Objective Study of Concept Formation', *Psychological Monographs* 42 (1932), no. 4 (whole no. 191).

3 S.C. Fisher, 'The Process of Generalising Abstraction: And Its Product, the General Concept', *Psychological Monographs* 21 (1916), no. 2 (whole no. 90).

4 See, for more experiments, R.R. Bush and F. Mosteller, 'A Model for Stimulus Generalization and Discrimination', *Psychological Review* LVIII (1951), pp. 413–23; and R.N. Shepard, C.I. Hovland and H.M. Jenkins, 'Learning and Memorization of Classifications', *Psychological Monographs* 75 (1961), no. 517.

5 Any equivalents given, that is, the practical limitations of scientific realism. Even if isosceles triangles were Fred Bloggs's favourite shapes, it would be unhelpful and potentially misleading to express (3) as 'They all possess the information that Fred Bloggs's favourite shape is the distinguishing feature.' We should think here rather of the common equivalences of the sort

derivable from dictionaries. Fred Bloggs's aesthetic tastes have no relevance to scientific explanation; although any extensionally equivalent substitution for (3) will express a *truth* about the subjects, not all truths are scientifically interesting.

6 The difficulty noted earlier of specifying what is to count as 'the same action' is not being neglected, and will shortly be discussed.

7 These three are cited by M.J. Levy in his *The Structure of Society*, (Princeton, 1952).

8 The assumption is that such a view of a purposive agent is comprehensive enough to embrace all, or almost all, of the goal-directed behaviour of a person. From recognising patterns to running a government – without stretching the language unduly – most actions can be called problem-solving. Perhaps such an assumption will not prove completely adequate; but it is more than enough to begin with.

9 W. Kalke, 'What is Wrong with Fodor and Putnam's Functionalism', *Nous*, III (1969), pp. 83–94.

10 Indeed, Nagel prefers to treat what I call the *G* and *R* categories as a single category: see his *The Structure of Science: Problems in the Logic of Scientific Explanation* (New York, 1961), pp. 527f. Others, like myself, prefer two categories; see C.G. Hempel, 'The Logic of Functional Analysis', in his *Aspects of Scientific Explanation* (New York, 1965), pp. 306f.

11 For a fuller discussion of this point, see Kalke, *op. cit.*

12 See N. Geschwind, 'Anatomy and the Higher Functions of the Brain', *Boston Studies in the Philosophy of Science*, vol. IV, pp. 98–136.

13 Such a claim usually provokes accusations of illicit anthropomorphisation of the brain. I have tried to rebut such arguments in 'Anthropomorphism and Analogy in Psychology', *Philosophical Quarterly*, XXV (1975), pp. 126–37, and shall not repeat the defence here.

CHAPTER 5

ROBOTS AND RESEARCH

I CONCLUDE from the previous chapter that intensionality is no barrier to physicalism. But physicalism may yet be untenable. There is a battery of further objections, all claiming, but usually for slightly different reasons, the inadequacy in principle of any psychophysiological account of a person; these form a messy set of arguments various in strength and importance. Fortunately the debate can be focused by a dash of science, of science fiction, and even of science fantasy. For the opponents and defenders of physicalism alike can and do express these new disagreements in terms of what we would, could, or should say about the intellectual capacities of artefacts constructed to simulate human performance. In this chapter I examine what contribution, if any, robots or computers can make to the debate over physicalism.

We must make one important preliminary distinction. The artefacts in question are all constructed to simulate some kind of human behaviour – to perform tasks that have hitherto been predominantly the preserve of human agency. But there are two completely distinct means to this end, and two equally distinct further purposes for which this end is sought. One kind of artefact attempts to simulate human performance by simulating as well whatever processes or procedures are thought to be used by humans or their brains; and the purpose of this enterprise is to gain greater understanding of how the brain works, by testing out a particular theory of its operation in a computer that models the theory. An altogether different kind of device is designed solely to model the products of human intelligence, and not the processes in the brain which bring them about. To construct devices that can perform some tasks hitherto restricted to humans, but perform them with superior speed and efficiency, is the goal here. Speed and efficiency often mean that processes quite different from those found in the human brain are used in the computer;[1] an ordinary pocket calculator provides an obvious illustration. Artefacts that try to simulate process as well as product, I shall call 'S' (simulation) robots or computers, and those concerned solely with the outcome will be designated 'AI' (artificial intelligence) robots or computers.

Now for the objections to physicalism. Opponents of physicalism usually argue for at least part of the following complex claim. Robots or computers may be constructed to model certain kinds of human behaviour, such as chess-playing. But the computer cannot literally be said to play chess – playing chess is *inter alia* a form of enjoyment, of intellectual challenge, of relaxation, or of entertainment, and for a computer none of these fuller descriptions of chess-playing could apply. The reason they do not apply is that computers can model only those human abilities that may be broken down into steps, abilities to perform tasks for which a stage-by-stage programme can be written. Enjoying something, relaxing, being entertained, and the like are not tasks or doings at all; hence they are not programmable tasks or doings. No amount of tinkering with its programme will enable a computer to simulate these unprogrammable but fundamental capacities of human beings. Similarly, one cannot programme a computer to want to win, to dislike losing, to hope an opponent fails to notice its exposed bishop; yet we must be able to apply some set of predicates of this kind if 'plays chess' is to be literally applicable, since our use of 'plays chess' loosely presupposes that there are some such further descriptions of the player. In short, 'is programmed to ϕ' nearly always licenses the inference 'doesn't really ϕ'. An adding machine doesn't really add any more than an abacus does; it is a programmed tool used by humans in their computations. It cannot genuinely be described as 'adding', because further descriptions of it such as 'having an aim or end in view', 'recognising its steps as steps of a calculation', 'choosing a strategy', 'hesitating', or 'getting a sudden insight', all of which are examples of the further predicates we must be able to apply to one who is genuinely adding, are all inappropriate and inapplicable. More generally, none of the *sentient* sides of human capacity can be modelled, only certain *sapient* performances such as step-by-step problem-solving; yet every time we can correctly apply some 'sapient' predicate it is necessary that we are also able to apply some 'sentient' predicates. So no psychological predicates at all can correctly be applied to computers. What is more, since sentience cannot be modelled there will be many problem-solving tasks that cannot be modelled by any computer, for there are several otherwise programmable tasks that explicitly require sentience: a computer that could successfully grade satsumas or satin would nevertheless be unable to rank stimuli on the pleasurable-painful spectrum. So computers are useless as models. Their limited ability to simulate some kinds of human behaviour provides no analysis or explanation of human adding or chess-playing, since they are not adding or playing chess; still less are they 'choosing' or 'deciding'; least of all can they be used to help explain intelligence, rationality, and consciousness. Finally, all currently designed computers are discrete-state digital systems. Since they are so − constructed from an assortment of physical parts which interact to move the system into one or another of a finite number of unambiguously describable distinct states – they must operate by breaking down every problem into a set of atomic sub-tasks, and advance single step by single step towards the conclusion. But we know that the human brain operates with many analogical processes – processes in which one cannot unambiguously identify any discrete states – hence it can often tackle problems in Gestalt fashion. For example, compare a computer's 'recognition' of a horse with a human's recognition: the computer must run seriatim through its finite checklist of characteristically equine features, whereas the human 'just recognises' a horse. This crucial difference is well highlighted by the continuing failure to produce a computer capable of recognising typographically various tokens of a letter, such as 'A'; we cannot find to feed into the computer a finite list of all the possible typological variations that still count as an A. So pattern-recognition, acknowledged to be one of the most fundamental of all human capacities, is a capacity that discrete-state systems seem incapable of simulating efficiently. In conclusion, if an artefact cannot be ascribed all the psychological predicates that we are prepared to ascribe to humans – and the claim is that it can be ascribed none – then it cannot explain the human capacities to which those predicates refer. If the artefact has been built to realise a functionalist model of human behaviour, then that model must be equally inadequate. And every such model is and must be inadequate, for the reasons given.

Underlying such an argument as this is the assumption that if no artefact can be given all the psychological predicates we are prepared to ascribe to humans, physicalism must be false. This assumption is at least questionable. We must point out at once that any unwillingness we may feel to ascribe psychological predicates to an *AI* computer is irrelevant, for the capacities or incapacities of such artefacts have no bearing upon the question of the adequacy of a specific psychophysiological theory of human functioning. It is S computers that must be in question. Perhaps it does seem plausible to suppose that if there were a complete psychophysiological theory of human functioning, then it should be possible to construct an S computer in accordance with this theory; and such a computer would have to model adequately *all* the capacities of human beings, if the physicalist theory is indeed comprehensive. But we should be cautious about this 'all'. In previous chapters we have plotted the ambitions of psychophysiology, and concluded that what it was seeking to explain were the most pervasive and fundamental human capacities, which it described in its own technical vocabulary. These capacities were required for the explanation of more complex activities, but the complex activities themselves were not the primary objects of analysis. We denied at some length that physicalism should seek to explain our use of ordinary-language mental terms. If the earlier arguments hold good, there will be no direct objection to physicalism in the argument that computers may not be ascribed our entire battery of *mental* concepts. We should remember, too, that in ascribing mental concepts we do not aim exclusively to describe and explain, but that we use them also to hint, to sneer, to rebuke, to warn, to congratulate, to console – the choice of terms is as much a function of our attitude to the subject as of that subject's behaviour. And clearly our attitude to a computer which we suspect, rightly or wrongly, of challenging our monopoly of personhood will be erratic and variable in the extreme: how we choose to describe it, and what psychological predicates we withhold, may depend far more upon our psychology than upon the computer's.

Nevertheless we cannot simply dismiss the objection as

misconceived, on the ground that it mistakes the ambition of physicalism by appealing to mental rather than psychological terms. It does make this mistake; but on the other hand it denies that *any* psychological (or mental) term can be ascribed to computers, and moreover highlights a serious omission in our account of physicalism as so far set forth. Up till now we have described physicalism as concerned solely with human action; about human experience it seems to be silent. Functionalism may look capable of explaining the human agent *qua* problem-solver, yet it has said nothing to help us understand how he can be a subject of experience too – how he feels pain and hunger, emotion and desire. Sapience but not sentience has been studied; yet the ultimate goal of explaining human rationality and intelligence must require an account of human sentience. Even if one grants that the ordinary-language mental terms like 'pain', 'hunger', 'emotion', etc., must not as such feature in the conceptual apparatus of the psychophysiological theory, some correlative terms, 'purified' for the purposes of science, must. For the ordinary-language explanation of actions in terms of belief has been transformed into the scientific explanation of certain forms of problem-solving behaviour in terms of information and other such notions; so analogously the ordinary-language descriptions and explanations of human experience and emotion require some corresponding account in psychophysiological terms. To say that computers could never be conscious or sentient is just to object that the physicalist theory as so far sketched has failed to account for such phenomena in *any* terms.

Thus there remains an extensive objection to the viability of psychophysiology, an objection focused by discussion of the alleged incapacities of computers. We cannot rebut the general charge against physicalism until we have examined the concepts of consciousness, sentience, and experience in chapter

6; but here we can prepare the way for that discussion by concentrating solely upon computer intelligence, its uses and limitations.

Is it true – no matter how we decide to analyse the concepts of experience and consciousness – that we should never be willing to ascribe terms of this kind to any artefact? The answer cannot be simple. We must grant the truism that an S computer can be programmed to perform only those tasks for which a programme can be written. Hence it will be impossible to write a programme that would 'make' an S computer feel pain, emotion, or hunger: these are not the things we do but things we suffer, and there is no 'way in which' we do them. We should concede also that some 'non-programmable' ascriptions may be required for many 'programmable' ascriptions to be legitimate – a computer that cannot feel pain indeed cannot be described as ranking stimuli on the pleasurable-painful spectrum. Nevertheless the fact that we cannot *programme* a computer to do something unprogrammable does not as yet entail that the computer cannot truly be ascribed non-programmable capacities. We have to ask how it is that we ascribe them to humans, and upon what grounds. For example, one necessary condition for legitimate pain-ascription may well be that the subject of ascription is a multicellular biochemical entity; hence our artefact, if it is to be a candidate subject of pain-ascriptions, would have to be constructed from synthesised protoplasm-like stuff. (Analogously, as things are, humans, unlike computers, cannot rust. But a few relatively minor modifications to our physical structure would enable us to share this unprogrammable ability with them.) A robot constructed from synthesised cells is not beyond the bounds of science fiction. The point is that some predications of psychological terms may require the artefact's hardware rather than its programme to be modified; tinkering with, and scrutinising, the programme cannot settle the question of the possibility of artificial sentience.[2]

The objection included another ground for denying that robots could experience pain, in claiming that they could not be thought to have desires, preferences, or values. This would mean that they could not be said to choose something, to prefer one thing to another, or to dislike anything; they may be programmed to select A rather than B when both A and B are available, but this selection could not be called 'their' preference or choice. This being so, no damage to a robot (even to a robot constructed from synthetic protoplasm-like stuff) would count as pain — for the crucial elements of desiring and preferring to avoid pain, dislike and fear of it, would be wholly missing. Briefly, robots may be caused to avoid dangerous situations, but could not have reasons for avoiding pain. A parallel argument would work for emotions, moods, and the like.

Again the argument becomes less convincing if we let in science fantasy. One might take a 'baby' robot — a robot before any programming has been done — and give it the following minimal programme. It is programmed to build its own programme; and to give a very high priority to certain goals, such as that of self-preservation. (It is probably obvious that I suggest we write in to the 'baby' robot's minimal programme analogues of all the instinctual drives that we assume to be part of a human infant's genetic and evolutionary endowment.) Then we allow it to develop its own programme in a social community, either among other equally sophisticated but 'adult' robots, or among people. How its self-programming works out will be largely conditioned by its initial programming — it is unlikely, for example, to place a very high priority upon notably dangerous activities, whereas it must give considerable weight to the needs of its body (whatever they may be). Further, it will learn from the society what that society values and what it rejects; and it is improbable that it would give high priority to anti-social behaviour, as the social sanctions that result, such as imprisonment, would frustrate its pursuit of the goals to which it has given high priority. It is, let us suppose, constructed from synthesised cells, so it has an analogue to our central nervous system, pain-receptors and all; moreover, there is no reason to assume that it is a discrete-state system (for we are talking of science fantasy, not fact), and so we can allow that its 'brain' may employ analogic as well as digital procedures. In short, if we make it sufficiently human in appearance, we may not be able to tell it apart from humans. For by hypothesis the infant robot at 'birth' is precisely on a par with the human infant; and further arguments are required to show that there must come a point at which it parts company with its human twin. But if we cannot tell it apart, then we have no grounds left for denying it sentience.

It is no good insisting that our robot does not *really* love and hate, enjoy Picasso, prefer raspberries to strawberries, choose, get irritated, and so forth. To insist upon insulating such attributions with scare-quotes is to express a prejudice, not to construct an argument. We should demand justification for such a clumsiness of grammar; and we must point out that we have no alternative way of describing or explaining the robot's ordinary behaviour − all that is true of the everyday explanation of human actions holds *pari passu* for the robot. Psychophysiological explanations will, as ever, suffice only to explain its possession of certain fundamental and pervasive capacities, not one of its unique and complex social actions; to predict or explain this we will need the apparatus of common-sense explanations. (Indeed, even today there are computers which we need to treat to some extent as though they were human; a sure way to lose a game against a chess-playing computer is to attempt to work out from its design and structure what moves it will make – the time required to do this would be far greater than any referee would allow. One might win if one treated it somewhat as one would a human opponent, working out its probable next move by ascribing to it plans and beliefs.) The only justification for insulating psychological attributions in scare-quotes would be a marked difference between our use of the terms for robots and our use of the terms for humans, and by hypothesis there is no such difference in our science fantasy. Where there is no difference, scare-quotes are as useless as Wittgenstein's stroke:[3]

> If someone taught me the word 'bench', and said that he sometimes or always put a stroke over it thus: 'bench', and that this meant something to him, I should say: 'I don't know what sort of idea you associate with this stroke, but it doesn't interest me unless there is a use for this stroke in the kind of calculus in which you wish to use the word "bench".'

Science fantasy may, then, describe coherently an artefact that has all or most of the properties of sentience and sapience. But science fantasy is infrequently useful in science, and so it proves here; the S robot described above obviously could teach us nothing, as we could not have constructed it unless we knew all we needed to know in the first place. We should not know anything more about it than we know about humans; scientifically speaking it would be an expensive and useless toy. Philosophically speaking it would pose fascinating problems for theories of personal identity, but it is not interesting in the context of the mind-body problem. All we have achieved by this fantasy is to rebut certain arguments against the logical possibility of such a robot; we may as well have continued to argue directly for the logical possibility of physicalism.

To discover the genuine role of computer simulation, we

must revert from science fantasy to science fact — revert to examining actual scientific practice. Here we find nothing in the least like the robot sketched above. Instead we have discrete-state digital computers with very limited abilities indeed; rarely would their creators wish to call them 'conscious' or 'intelligent'; in fact many a scientist working with such artefacts may agree with the entire content of the objection cited on pages 69–71 above. What then is the point of these limited S computers, and why do physicalists find them interesting? Answering this question will show us why the objection cited entirely misses the point of research in computer simulation of brain function.

Once again we need to consider the functionalist method. It will often happen that a number of distinct and competing functional hypotheses (sets of r's) may be derived from a study of, and rival each other in explaining, particular types of problem-solving behaviour. We need some method for testing them, to enable us to select (albeit tentatively, while awaiting corroboration or refutation from neurophysiological research) what seems to be the most promising of the hypotheses. In some domains of study, notably in the psychophysiology of perception, hypotheses can be directly tested by examining frog, cat, or monkey brains; and occasionally the effects of lesions in human brains can be studied, and may provide evidence that bears upon a particular functional hypothesis. But usually direct examination of the living human brain is impossible, so the evidence available for corroborating or falsifying competing hypotheses is meagre and inconclusive. We simply lack the necessary neurophysiological data. Thus there is a demand for an heuristic intermediary between the molar levels and the micro-levels of analysis: and this is typically found by feeding one of the suggested functional hypotheses into a computer, and attempting to simulate the *analysandum* g in terms of the functional hypothesis about the *r*'s. In other words, from the functional hypothesis offered by the psychologist one derives an abstract model of the workings of the system *S* in the form of a flow chart, the output of which will be the various members of *G* under consideration, the input a description of the problem. In between will be structural items (*x*'s) to perform the functions (*r*'s) that are postulated (such as 'selecting information', 'analysing stimulus-input', and so forth), giving due allowance to desiderata such as cross-checking or negative-feedback processes. The aim is to provide a model that has sufficient neurophysiological as well as psychological implications to serve as a bridge between the data and conjectures of psychology on the one hand and those of neurophysiology on the other. What one is modelling will only be a part of the human behaviour that is currently under study (a chess-playing computer does not have hands with which to move the pieces); and the behaviour under study may itself be a highly specific, restrictively specified, *g*. It is essential, therefore, to have a clear grasp of what the *g*'s in question are, so that one knows what the model is not expected to do as well as what it is.

There are several dimensions of assessment in terms of which we can evaluate the comparative merits of a selection of computer simulations: these dimensions should not be confused. First, there is the dimension of accuracy: when simulating a particular kind of problem-solving behaviour, the better computer is one which reproduces the *g*'s that the human subject produces when handling that problem. Not only should it simulate observed human behaviour in a reliable way; ideally it should have efficient predictive power too, and reflect what a human would do with a new example of that kind of problem. In sum, computer *A* will be considered to realise a less profitable or plausible model of brain function than computer *B* if B simulates more accurately within the same domain, echoing actual human performance more exactly.

However, the triumph of B may be temporary and limited; for there is a second dimension of assessment to consider, in terms of which one would prefer a third computer C which simulates all that B does and related tasks as well. As an illustration, suppose that B is a chess-playing computer. If C can perform as well, or nearly as well, as B in its simulation of chess-playing, but can also play draughts, backgammon, and chequers, it is to be preferred. For as observed on p. 63 above, we are searching for an economical set of r's and x's to explain the maximum amount of behaviour; the functional hypothesis realised in computer C explains a greater range of human performance than does that realised in B, so it is reasonable to suppose that C has a greater functional isomorphism with a human agent than does B. We may hope to replace C, in turn, by a computer that is capable of yet more tasks.

An interesting and important third dimension of assessment concerns the depth of the functional isomorphism achieved by any simulation. This requires us to look and see how far down the ramifying hierarchies of r's the man/machine isomorphism spreads. The notion of 'functional isomorphism' needs careful spelling out. Just as a model is designed to simulate aspects of restricted types of behaviour and not to model all aspects of human behaviour at once, so the claim that it does so 'in the same way' must be made with reference to a pragmatically given standard. Consider again the mundane washing machine, S_m. In one sense it washes clothes (g_m) 'in the same way' as a man doing his laundry, i.e. by soaking (r_1), soaping (r_2), rinsing (r_3), and drying (r_4) them. But such isomorphism is not very informative, holding as it does only for general and broadly described functions. Once we break up $r_1, \ldots, r_4$ and consider how the washing machine fulfils these, we discover new and more detailed r's, such as 'tumbling', 'agitating', and 'spinning'. Here the functional isomorphism breaks down, for a man is not so constructed as to be able to tumble and spin clothes; and impressed by this difference, we should probably conclude that the washing machine does not after all wash clothes in the same way as a man. Whether we say it does or it doesn't will depend upon which g and r descriptions we are taking: clearly some will be heuristically far more valuable than others. An hypothesis about human behaviour, postulating that the human agent performs task T by analysing input, processing information, and so forth, might well be realised in a computer performing T by those same means; yet once the r processes of analysing input, etc., are dissected into their constituent functions, all isomorphism may then be lost. A computer that is functionally isomorphic to the human agent at only a general level will be far less useful than one capable of more detailed functional isomorphisms. The question 'Done in the same way?' must be asked again and again, at each level in the hierarchy of r's; that the answer may be 'Yes' at a global level has no bearing on what it may be at a more detailed level.

A related fourth dimension of assessment is that of structural isomorphism. No amount of functional isomorphism could entail, or even show to be probable, a conclusion about structural isomorphism; for, as described in chapter 4 (pp. 61–3), there is no definite cut-off point in the specification of r's at which members of X can be relied upon to appear and fulfil them. In a system S_1, the functions r_1 and r_2 may be performed by x_1 and x_2 respectively; but in S_2 the same r_1 may need dissection into r_a, r_b, and r_c, which in turn initiate a search for adequate x's; and r_2 may not need dissection into more detailed r's, but may meet its structural realisation in, say, x_a and x_b, or x_c and x_d. A simple illustration: a computer may have three complex structural units, an input processor (x_1), an information store (x_2), and a selector mechanism (x_3), which perform the r's of interpreting input (r_1), storing information (r_2), and selecting action-routines (r_3); but it is certain that no human brain will display on examination three such handily discrete and morphologically identifiable neurophysiological structures. Whenever a set of r's seems to be isomorphic in man and machine, the question of isomorphism can be raised about their realisations.

In the light of the last two points we should realise that if we persist with the questions 'Done in the same way?' and 'Done by the same kinds of micro-entities?' we shall eventually reach a stage where the answer in each case has to be negative, so long as we are comparing the performances of humans and discrete-state, mechanical, S computers. The reason, evidently, is that computers are not multicellular biochemical organisms, people are; and there must come a point at which the difference tells. Indeed it is already apparent that computer simulation is not heuristically valuable as a research tool in any detailed study of the processes of memory storage; the evidence is mounting that the storage of information in the brain requires a synthesis of protein and nucleic acid in the cells, so that memory must be in part a matter of subtle changes in nerve-cell chemistry and structure, changes which alter the probability of a particular nerve cell firing. Computer simulation of this chemical transaction could scarcely throw new light upon it. Again, computers store information 'bits' in conceptualised form – in ALGOL or FORTRAN or some other code – whereas the human brain does not. At least, we may call the brain's storage a 'coded' storage if we choose, but the 'code' in question is like no natural or artificial language. Each brain will have its own unique 'code'; because which neurons fire, and in what combinations, when the brain receives a particular stimulus input, will depend upon the immediately preceding nerve-cell firings (for neurons have a rest period after firing). Since this is so, and since there are 10^{10} neurons in the human brain, the chances of cross-brain identity in the cellular storage of a single item of information will be considerably less likely than an identity of fingerprints. Indeed, as Dennett has noted,[4] it would be perverse to expect or want information to be stored in the brain in syntactically analysable form; it would set us upon a regress in which we should need to postulate systems and mechanisms to 'read' and 'understand' this language, and hence with their own mechanisms for storing, translating, and processing information. Information is indeed stored in computers in syntactically analysable form, but this is only because human language-users so encoded it, and will themselves subsequently decode it.[5]

We must acknowledge, then, that computer simulation of many micro-functions will be impossible because of the need for multicellular biochemical structures to fulfil them. (This failure of S computers may perhaps be remedied when more results come in from the work being done on artefacts constructed of synthesised cells; here I am concerned solely with the bulk of the research that goes by the name of 'computer simulation', research that employs mechanical artefacts.) Yet despite this essential limitation of any non-biochemical simulating device, one can envisage a computer which allowed an affirmative answer to the questions 'Done in the same way?', and 'Done by the same kinds of micro-entities?' asked of each of a descending hierarchy of structures and functions until a micro-level of brain structure is reached; and with that, most of the battle would be won. For in that particular structural-functional analysis of that specific bit of behaviour, a bridge would have been built between the data and the theories of the experimental psychologists, and the data and the theories of the neurophysiologists. Computer simulation is so heuristic, so suggestive, and such a powerful tool — both actually and potentially — for research into brain function that it deserves to be counted as an intrinsic and indispensable part of psychophysiological methodology. That a given simulation must, like an instance of Marxian dialectic, be discarded, transcended, or absorbed once its task is done is no slight upon it, for this is precisely the role of the model: to be tested, to suggest the course of further simulations, and eventually to be found wanting, once it has enabled the researcher to progress beyond it to the study of functions more complex than those it has been devised to model. Without computer simulation, psychological theory would founder before it had effected any solid link with the theoretical structure of neurophysiology.

We can now see why the objection described near the beginning of this chapter is wholly irrelevant to current research into S computers. One can grant that little research is done in the simulation of sentience; computer simulation is, simply, a poor tool for this area. It matters not at all that we may be reluctant to say of a computer that it is really playing chess, or planning a strategy, choosing, or even adding; one can model an X without being an X, just as a decoy duck models a duck but isn't a duck. Perhaps a computer that successfully models a very wide range of problem-solving behaviour may be entitled to have genuine psychological predicates ascribed to it; in the next chapter we examine what sorts of considerations *are* relevant for a range of psychological ascriptions. But even if it is not so entitled, its value as a research tool is entirely unaffected.

Notes

1 But for some purposes *AI* theorists study the human brain; whenever, in fact, cerebral processes seem speedier and more

efficient than any alternative. At present the structure and function of neural nets interest *AI* theorists particularly, as their efficiency surpasses that of any other device. So where humans are much better at certain tasks than are existing machines – as they are at recognising patterns – *AI* theorists become to some extent S theorists, albeit for different reasons.

2 For a fuller explanation and discussion of this point, see K. Gunderson, *Mentality and Machines* (New York, 1971), pp. 136–59.

3 L. Wittgenstein, *The Blue and Brown Books* (Oxford, 1964), p. 65.

4 D.C. Dennett, *Content and Consciousness* (London, 1969), pp. 86–7.

5 Most neurophysiologists would now accept the theory that the storage of an information 'bit' comes at the end of a long series of neural nets which filter out the 'noise', or irrelevant features, of the stimulus. For example, a peripheral neural net may fire only when presented with small round objects of uniform colour; another, only when the small round uniformly coloured objects are coins; and so on. Eventually a thoroughly interpreted stimulus-input can be matched against traces of past stimuli in the information storage system. The process of interpretation will be a continuous one from the peripheral receptors to neural nets deep in the brain. It is the action the organism takes upon receiving such stimuli that determines (a) what patterns regularly get interpreted – for regular usage confirms and establishes the neural linkages, thus raising the probability of subsequent firings; and (b), how we might hope to 'crack the neural code' – to find the significance, for that organism, of various neural firing patterns. This theory has received good support from the study of the perceptual mechanisms of frogs and cats. See J.J. Gibson, *The Senses Considered As Perceptual Systems* (London, 1968); D.H. Hubel and T.N. Wiesel, 'Receptive Fields and Functional Architecture in Two Nonstriate Visual Areas (18 and 19) of the Cat', *Journal of Neurophysiology*, 28 (1965), pp. 229–89; and J.Y. Lettvin, H.R. Maturana, W.S. McCulloch and W.H. Pitts, 'What the Frog's Eye Tells the Frog's Brain', *Proceedings of the Institute of Radio Engineers*, 47 (1959), pp. 1,940–51.

CHAPTER 6

SENSATIONS AND SENTIENCE

I N the preceding chapter we noted that our physicalist theory, the theory of psychophysiological functionalism, has so far done nothing to explain the sentient capacities of human beings, has not shown how people can be conscious experiencers as well as agents. Although I argued that an S robot built on psychophysiological principles might prove to *be* conscious, I offered no indication of what physicalism might do to explain this feature − the robot's sentience was no more explained than was that of humans. We can see clearly what has yet to be analysed if we revert to the distinction drawn in chapter 1 between the question of the truth of monism, and the question of the viability of physicalism; for there it was argued that the debate over monism is typically viewed as the issue of the ontological status of subjective, experiential mental phenomena − precisely the phenomena with which physicalism is now confronted. Hence, although the problems of monism and physicalism are distinct, and should be kept distinct, the physicalist needs to come to terms with the subject matter of the monist's arguments.

When discussing earlier the issue of monism and the merits of the 'incorrigibility' criterion of the mental, we saw that the incorrigibility criterion failed to distinguish the class of mental phenomena adequately because, in so far as it marked anything at all, it characterised only occurrent, clockable, and sensation-like mental events − 'sentient' phenomena − but did not suit mental states like dispositions, moods, emotions, or the propositional attitudes of belief and desire − the 'sapient' mental states. This explained why the debate about the truth of monism, a thesis which presupposes that we have some individuated and reidentifiable mental events and processes to identify or correlate with physical events and processes, tended generally to employ the incorrigibility criterion to distinguish the mental half of its subject matter. The physicalist debate was rightly more concerned with those mental states marked by intensionality. But now physicalism is challenged to deal with just the mental phenomena that concern the monist; and so we should re-examine in greater detail the incorrigibility criterion, this time rather *qua* criterion of the sentient than *qua* criterion of the mental. Unfortunately, the incorrigibility criterion will again prove inadequate, even to the more limited task of picking out only the sentient mental states; but there is much to be learned from this failure, and we shall see where we ought to be looking for the realm of the sentient.

The incorrigibility criterion purports to identify sentient phenomena by requiring their possession of some or all of the following marks: they are private, subjective, phenomenal; a man's knowledge of his own sentient mental states is privileged, and his way of knowing is unlike that of an outsider; he has immediate or non-inferential knowledge of them; his sincere first-person present-tense reports on his experiences cannot in principle be overridden. Not all of these features deserve examination. 'Subjective', for example, is a much-abused term that has been used to mean practically anything about which there is room for a difference of opinion; and if we knew what 'phenomenal' meant we should already know what 'sentient', 'experiential', and 'consciousness' meant. But the tests of privacy, privileged or asymmetrical access, immediacy or non-inferentiality, and incorrigibility, can and have been studied, and must be studied again for any light they may shed upon the concept of consciousness.

First, privacy. Ayer has usefully distinguished[1] four main senses of 'private', none of which will give us a really independent or clear mark of sentient phenomena. The first and strongest sense of 'private' is that X is private to A if A alone, and not conceivably anyone else, could detect its existence. The absurdity and untenability of this suggestion are so well known that it should be passed over in silence: nothing is, nor ever could be, private in this sense. Second comes the sense of 'private' in which X is private to A if there is at least one way that A can detect X's existence in which B cannot. Now this sense of 'private' collapses into the notion of A's 'privileged', or 'asymmetrical', access to his own sensations, so we can postpone examination of it until we discuss privileged and asymmetrical access explicitly; although we might note in passing that many physical states, such as a full stomach, may be private in this sense. The third interpretation of 'private' that Ayer gives us is that X is private to A if A's authority concerning the existence or non-existence of X could not be overridden. This sense seems to provide a fairly clear criterion; but like the second sense, the criterion it offers is equivalent to that offered by another notion, this time that of incorrigibility, so we shall again postpone examination. Fourth and finally, X is private to A if A cannot share X with anyone else. This is the most complex interpretation of privacy, since 'share' itself can be given various meanings. There is a familiar sense of the term in which A cannot 'share' his passport, his birth certificate, his haircut, his build, his sleep, his frown, and many other non-mental possessions. Certainly there is another use of 'share' in which he can; we often do say that A and B have the same

build, the same frown, or the same haircut. But in this sense of
'same' and 'share', *A* and *B* can have the same headache, itch,
or ache. In short, the type-token ambiguity seems to pervade
mental and non-mental 'unshareables' indifferently. Further, it
seems nothing more than a contingent matter of fact that a pain
(for example) is in general treated as something unique to each
individual rather than as a shareable general phenomenon. We
might, for example, imagine a world in which headaches
behaved like fogs, never affecting one person without affecting
the entire population within a certain area. (This is easy enough
to imagine. As it is, many people in a particular geographical
region all experience a dull headache just before the onset of a
thunderstorm; if we imagined *everyone* in that region so
afflicted, we should have a 'headache fog'.) In such a world we
might have no use for talk of individual headaches any more
than we have now for talk of individual foggedness.
Alternatively we could imagine a world of telepaths, where *A*'s
pain was instantly felt by several others; in this world the
concept of pain might become more like the concept of weight,
where *A*'s weight is the same weight as *B*'s so long as they tip
the scales at the same figure. No analogy to the shareability or
unshareability of pain can be perfect − that is the nature of
analogies. But there are enough different analogies on offer to
make it clear that one cannot single out sentient phenomena as
'unshareable' in any sense of the word that is peculiar to them.

Privacy, then, provides no independent criterion of the
sentient. It either fails to distinguish experiential phenomena
from other things, or it adds nothing to the other criteria
offered. We turn next to the test of privileged access and to the
weaker form of this test, asymmetrical access. To say that *A* is
privileged about his experiential states is to say that he is in a
better position to judge of them than is *B*; to say he has
asymmetrical access to them is to say that his way of knowing

is *unlike* that of anyone else. Evidently it would usually be silly
to deny that a man has both privileged and asymmetrical access
to his own sentient states. For A's grounds for ascribing
sensations like pain to himself (if indeed it makes sense to speak
of him having 'grounds' at all) tend to be both unlike, and better
than, B's grounds for ascribing a pain to A. So we should allow
that at least the simple bodily sensations like twinges, tickles,
aches, and pains are generally matters of both privileged and
asymmetrical access. The test of privileged and asymmetrical
access is weakened in force, as was the test of the fourth sense
of 'private', by the logical possibility of extensive telepathy,
which would make B's access to A's pain indistinguishable to
A's access; and as we have already seen, some physical states
may get included by this criterion. Nevertheless, privileged
access serves as a pointer to the direction in which we need to
go.

Sometimes the privilege of the access is explained by citing
the 'immediacy', or 'non-inferentiality' of a person's knowledge
of his own experiential states − the next test offered by the
incorrigibility criterion. But so far from explaining privileged
access, the notions of immediacy and non-inferentiality merely
obscure what seems otherwise reasonably clear. Not all
sentient states are known without inference: pain usually is,
but one may need to work out whether a spot seen on the wall
is, or is not, an after-image. Further, we seem ready to allow
knowledge of things other than our own mental states to be
non-inferential. The awareness that one is standing, lying,
crossing one's legs, or trembling is not normally called
inferential; moreover, people can learn to report 'directly' upon
the presence of alpha-wave activity in the brain.[2] Facts
concerning external objects or other people can be known
immediately too: a scientist can realise without inference that
his cloud-chamber is malfunctioning, or a husband that his

wife is unhappy. Defenders of the immediacy mark of the
sentient will object that knowledge of one's physical states, of
malfunctioning cloud-chambers, or of another's unhappiness,
cannot really and truly be non-inferential — subconsciously one
must be utilising kinaesthetic evidence, subliminal perceptions,
or behavioural cues, and inferring from these. But this
objection cannot be maintained. If non-conscious 'inference' is
to count as inference for the purposes of the immediacy
criterion, then the neurophysiologist may legitimately point out
that complex transactions of which we are not conscious are
required for pain-recognition; perhaps we non-consciously
'infer' that we are in pain from non-consciously monitored
cerebral cues. Furthermore, the psychology of perception has
shown how difficult and implausible it is to try to isolate classes
of perceptions where no inferences of any kind come into play
— perception seems invariably to 'go beyond' the data of bare
stimulus-input. But if, on the other hand, only *conscious*
inference counts as inference for the purposes of the immediacy
mark of the sentient, then, first, we are begging the question, as
we have to assume that we already know the difference
between conscious and non-conscious states; and second,
people are often said to know without conscious inference
some of their physical states, some facts about the external
world, and some of the experiential states of another. There is
nothing suspect or dubious about the notions of immediate
awareness or non-inferential knowledge *per se*, though. The
fact of the matter is that the distinction between mediated and
unmediated or inferential and non-inferential knowledge is
important and useful; but the *useful* distinction is by no means
the same distinction as the absolute and rigid dichotomy
implicit in the incorrigibility criterion's sense of 'immediate'
and 'non-inferential'. The useful distinction is a contextually
variable one — different situations impose different standards, so

that what may pass as uninferred in an ordinary context may not so pass in a law-court. It is hard indeed to imagine situations in which sincere first-person, present-tense reports of experiential states would not count as uninferred, or immediate; but we no longer need to distinguish such cases by the philosophical fantasy of an absolute or metaphysically grounded immediacy. It is not hard to see why this absolute kind of immediacy was thought to be required: a particular epistemological theory required it. Faced by the epistemological sceptic, philosophers sought to rebut him by discovering a set of absolutely indubitable items of knowledge. Anything that was a candidate object of indubitable knowledge had to be known immediately and non-inferentially; for only if this relation of absolute directness held between knower and known would there be literally no room to squeeze in the logical possibility of error, would there be no link to be enfeebled by sceptical doubt. But now we no longer believe that the best or only way to rebut the extreme sceptic depends upon our finding absolutely or metaphysically indubitable foundations for our web of beliefs – we have other means of answering him, and I do not propose to assess their efficacy – and the need for a philosophically 'deep' indubitability has gone. With it vanishes the need to wrench terms like 'immediate' and 'non-inferential' away from their normal meaning and make them serve esoteric and specialised functions for a particular philosophical theory.

The foregoing remarks prepare one for the dismissal of 'incorrigibility' as a criterion of the experiential. Absolute incorrigibility is a will o' the wisp that we no longer need pursue. If we return to the word its everyday meaning – roughly, that A's sincere testimony about X is incorrigible if we have at present no evidence that we would regard as outweighing it – then most of our reports upon our contemporaneous sentient states will be incorrigible. This incorrigibility is no longer a metaphysically necessary or unalterable fact, but is instead a contingent and readily comprehensible reflection of the trust we place in certain kinds of evidence. Perhaps there never will be any evidence we would be willing to use that would override A's sincere testimony that he is in pain. But the possibility of such evidence is no longer ruled out in principle; further, 'He is in pain' may in certain circumstances count as incorrigible, as may many reports that are not reports on mental phenomena at all. 'Absolute' incorrigibility is required only by a foundationalist epistemology, just as only a particular Christian viewpoint requires the infallibility of *ex cathedra* pronouncements of the Pope; and philosophers, more fortunate than Catholic theologians, can now declare the need for such a problematic notion past.

The traditional marks of sentience, cited under the general heading 'the incorrigibility criterion', do not then serve to pick out unambiguously the range of mental phenomena with which physicalism still has to cope. Now, though, we can see more clearly why they could not serve. It is evident that any 'criterion' which describes sentient phenomena solely in terms of our epistemological relationship towards them may tell us very little about the sorts of thing to which we have this relationship; and further, the motive for introducing the incorrigibility criterion in the first place was *not* primarily to tell us anything about sentience, but rather to provide indubitable bits of knowledge that would serve to underpin the structure of human knowledge and belief. This is a conclusion to which we shall return in the next and final chapter.

It would seem, then, that it is a mistake to look for any neat and comprehensive 'mark' of sentience. (Certainly there is no *a priori* reason why there should be one.) The fact that the incorrigibility criterion fails, and that it is difficult or impossible to imagine any other criterion that would be successful in its stead, surely indicates that whatever else sentient phenomena may prove to be, they will not fall into a homogeneous class. We may be fairly sure that they will all be known in a privileged and incorrigible way (where 'privileged' and 'incorrigible' do not mean *logically* privileged and incorrigible); other than that, we shall have to rely on intuition and examine paradigm cases of experiential states — those about which all can agree.

If we do this, we find as predicted a thoroughly heterogeneous bunch of states; to reduce them to some order I propose to sort them into two kinds. The first kind is the class of sensations: occurrent bodily sensations such as pains, aches, tingles, twitches, itches. The second kind comprises all those mental states in which we are aware of something that is *not* a bodily sensation. (I realise of course that 'awareness' is no help in the analysis of consciousness, as it is practically synonymous with it, and both terms need fuller treatment.[3] Here, however, we are explicitly relying on intuition and are treating only paradigm cases, so that we can exclude problem cases and limit the discussion to just those mental states where we can all agree that there is awareness.) This class would include items like A's seeing the redness of a sunset, his knowing that his left leg is bent, his awareness that he is reaching a decision or is remembering Vienna, and so on. These objects of awareness do not presuppose that A needs any occurrent bodily sensations or specific experiences of a sensation-like sort. I shall call the first kind of conscious experience the 'intransitive' sentient states, the second, 'transitive'. Intransitive states are those where we think the object discriminated (e.g., a pain) does not exist independently of the discrimination of it, or in other words where the *esse* of the object is its *percepi*. 'Intransitive' is a useful label for this class, for whatever kind of sensation is in question, it is easy to imagine that the grammatically transitive *form* of the sensation report, i.e. 'I feel a pain', 'I have an itch', 'I'm forming a mental image of King's College chapel', could be changed into a grammatically transitive form, 'I'm in pain', 'I'm itching', 'I'm visualising King's College chapel'. Transitive sentient states, on the other hand, are such that the object discriminated may exist independently of the discrimination, so that no conversion into a grammatically intransitive form is possible. 'I see the sunset', which is there whether I see it or not; 'I am aware that my left leg is bent', as it might well be even when I am not aware of it; 'I have reached a decision', but I might have come to a decision without realising it. Ordinary sense perception, much kinaesthetic perception, and most kinds of self-consciousness, would fall into the transitive class.

The history of philosophy shows that it has been popular to try to assimilate the transitive conscious states to the intransitive ones. The motive is clear: only intransitive states have any chance of supporting logically incorrigible claims, and this incorrigibility was the main weapon deployed against the epistemological sceptic. Hence philosophers introduced into the analysis of sense experience intermediate perceptual entities, entities whose *esse* was to be *percepi*: sense impressions, sense data, qualia, sensa, 'raw feels'. Consciousness of the contents of one's own mind was made intransitive by fiat: to think just was to be aware that one was thinking; so also with deciding, remembering, planning, etc. This attempt to assimilate transitive to intransitive sentient states is a mistake, however understandable a mistake. For it ignores the fact that if one is trying to grasp the concepts of consciousness or sentience, it is no help to take an artificially distorted or technically defined concept as *analysandum* – that is to change the subject. Understanding what 'consciousness', 'sensation', 'experience' and the like mean in ordinary language requires an examination of the natural uses of these terms. And once these natural uses are considered, it emerges that the items we count as objects of experience are pains, itches, thoughts – and chairs, densities, sounds, hues. In other words, we naturally assume that the direct objects of sense experience are the *public* appearances of things. It is these we confront immediately and non-inferentially most of the time; when we describe or report upon such items all that is required is a mastery of the language. On the other hand, if we are asked to describe and report upon sense data rather than upon the way things look, we need to master a sophisticated technique and an esoteric vocabulary. We have to acquire a phenomenological attitude to our sense experience, and then employ technical concepts like 'sense datum' with which to describe it. That it is difficult to see one's sensory experience phenomenologically is now clear: if psychologists want to get people to see a coin as an elliptical brown patch, they have to make them look down a narrow tube at the coin, so that the perceptual cues from the surrounding environment which make it impossible to see the coin as anything but a coin are blanked out. And, outside the experimental context, we are all familiar with the fact that the naïve child who paints a face will paint it as a uniform pink; it requires the trained artist, who has succeeded in adopting the phenomenological attitude to what he paints, to depict the face by seeing and portraying the white, blue, green, or grey patches of shade or highlight on it. Not only is the technique for acquiring the phenomenological attitude a sophisticated one; the sense-datum terminology, too, seems full of difficulties. It is far from clear, for example, what counts as one sense datum and what as two; whether sense data can be complex; whether they can recur; how long they last; and so on. However, my main aim here is not to attack sense-datum theory, but rather to point out that it is not only difficult and implausible, but also entirely unnecessary, to restrict sentience to intransitive mental states. The attempt so to restrict it is due, again, to the demands of foundationalist epistemology and its search for the logically incorrigible. We can now re-state the reason why the incorrigibility criterion of the sentient does and must fail: it fails precisely because it excludes all transitive conscious states. Torn between the need to represent conscious experience as that of which we are directly aware (in an everyday sense of 'directly'), and the need to represent it as something about which we are logically incorrigible, philosophers were driven by the threat of the epistemological sceptic to succumb to the latter; but they gave a despairing hand-wave to the former by pretending that the hitherto innocuous phrase 'directly aware' was in fact equivalent to the portentous technical notion of absolute immediacy. But so far from being equivalent, the two prove to be incompatible: the objects of 'absolutely immediate' awareness do not resemble even remotely those of ordinary direct awareness.

We can, then, keep to the distinction between transitive and intransitive sentient states. This gives us one class consisting of sensations proper, like pains, itches, and tingles, and a second class comprising sense experience, much kinaesthetic experience, and our awareness, when indeed we have it, of our own mental processes. Now we can consider how physicalism is to cope with sentience, beginning with the intransitive states and then moving on to the bigger question of the transitive ones.

I shall follow the general custom of taking pain as a clear and paradigmatic instance of all bodily sensations, and discuss intransitive conscious experiences in terms of this paradigm. The challenge to physicalism, then, is to explain how it is that humans feel pain; and a useful preliminary question is: In what circumstances, to what entities, and why, are we willing to ascribe pain sensations?

It is most significant that our intuitions are wholly unclear and notably inconsistent when we are thinking of ascribing pain to any but the higher animals. Most are prepared to agree that dogs and dolphins, cats and cows, feel pain; yet there is no consensus about fish, reptiles, insects, amoebae, or even plants. But what does emerge clearly is that animals that (most of us would agree) have indeed the capacity for pain experience are all animals with a central nervous system of some complexity; and there is a clue in this. If we consider an organism with a comparatively simple nervous system, like an amoeba, we know that it has very limited sensory and motor capacities. It can move slowly towards and away from things, can absorb nourishment, can discriminate heat and coldness, extremes of light or dark. Probably it has other important capacities, too − my knowledge of amoebae is limited − but the point remains that it can do little and sense little. In other words, the world of an amoeba is not complex at all, for its world consists only of those things which it is capable of distinguishing, and these are very few. Hence stimuli that people discriminate, and discriminate as painful (like the touch of a nettle), are not registered by their sensory apparatus, do not affect them at all, and no avoidance behaviour is required. There is indeed a tiny number of distinct sorts of stimuli that could be registered by an amoeba as threatening; perhaps extremes of heat and light, great water-turbulence, or dryness, but little else.

With so few discrete kinds of threat, and with a motor capacity as limited as the sensory, the amoeba has, in the face of danger, the options of moving (slowly) or staying put. Perhaps the threat of hot water requires movement away; whereas the threat of turbulent water is best met by staying put and clinging tight. The physicalist who seeks to explain these activities needs to postulate no more than that amoebae have genetically endowed reflex reactions to distinct stimuli (reactions strictly parallel to our patellar reflex). The explanation would be completely adequate; to suppose as well that the amoeba experienced pain from the hot water would be unnecessary. One can account for behaviour that is a reaction to a threat without postulating a mediating sensation, if one can show that the reception of the stimuli that signal danger automatically triggers off the appropriate reaction.

By contrast, the higher animals with their sophisticated nervous systems have a vastly greater range of both sensory and motor abilities. Since their sense organs discriminate far more distinct phenomena (i.e. since different patterns of neurons fire when distinguishable types of stimuli are received) their world is much richer, more complex, and more varied than is that of the lower animals. Among the items present to them in this detailed environment will be many diverse kinds of potentially dangerous or beneficial elements, which will demand attention and action. Corresponding to the diversity of these objects of choice or avoidance, the animal's action and reaction techniques must be sophisticated, flexible, and modifiable, appropriate to the specific combinations of threatening or advantageous objects discriminated. They need, in short, an extensive and alterable behavioural repertoire: and this need precludes the possibility that they could get by with the inbuilt and stereotyped reflexes which suffice for lower life-forms. (In principle, of course, all animals might have inherited at birth a comprehensive repertoire of reflex reactions, apt for all the situations that demanded a response; but a vast brain capacity would be required to contain all these reflex mechanisms, and even then small changes in the environment, creating a novel stimulus, might prove disastrous as there would be no reaction tailored to fit the stimulus.) Thus to explain the behaviour of these animals requires more than was required to account for that of an amoeba: but there is a simple

and economical way to do it. We postulate a capacity that
mediates between stimulus and response, the capacity for pain
sensation. Pain serves as an indication of danger or threat to the
survival of the organism: animals can learn to adopt, adapt, or
reject an action-routine on the basis of one (painful) false move.
Once bitten, twice shy; sensations of pain are admirably
tailored to cut short the lengthy and risky attainment of
adaptive reaction by evolution's blind trial-and-error method.

Now pain, here being considered as a signal of danger or
threat to the health and survival of the organism, involves
damage to, or malfunctioning of, the body; for the creature's
safety is threatened by injuries such as a cut, a sprain, or a
blow. Nerves carry the signals of damage back to the brain
which, on the basis of the immediate environment, can initiate
appropriate compensatory activity, and if necessary, adjust it to
further changes in the situation. This presupposes not only
sophisticated sensory and motor abilities. It presupposes also
that we can attribute to the organism a drive or instinct for
survival; for pain would have no rationale, *qua* signal of
danger, unless the animal had such a drive. The physicalist will
not be impressed by the objection that there is no reason why
pain *should* have a rationale – that we might experience pain
even if we were constitutionally incapable of profiting from it.
He deals with facts rather than with logical possibilities. And
the facts are that pain is known to play a critical role in the
preservation of life – those rare unfortunates who are incapable
of feeling pain have to be watched night and day to ensure that
they do not endanger themselves by gulping boiling liquids,
leaving untended cuts to turn gangrenous, or sleeping in a
position that strains the muscles; and they infrequently survive
to old age. Moreover, there is a sufficient backlog of biological,
zoological, and entomological evidence in support of the
Aristotelian adage that nature does nothing in vain, to convince

us that pain should not arbitrarily be treated as exceptional. It may not be part of the concept of pain that it is useful; but psychophysiology is not concerned with conceptual analysis.

Pain receptors, then, detect bodily damage and malfunctioning; nerves carry this message to the brain where characteristic patterns of neural firing result; for such a process to happen *is* for the organism to experience pain. By saying this, the physicalist has become a monist. But this 'is' should not be thought to import a thesis of a strong or Leibnizian identity of pains and brain processes. The question whether or not monism requires identity is, as we saw in chapter 1, something no scientist should nor could attempt to establish − his aim is explanation. Scientific research cannot produce an iota of evidence for identifying pains with brain processes that is not also, to precisely the same extent, evidence for (for example) the incompatible dualist thesis of parallelism. Certainly the physicalist wants to argue for monism of *some* kind − for if parallelism held true, there would be the amazing brute fact of a mental-physical coincidence that would be inexplicable in physical terms; but his best bet is to avoid the entire identity dispute.

He can avoid it by adopting the view described as 'having all the advantages of theft over honest toil', the view known as Eliminative Materialism.[4] This gives one an unqualified monism that dodges and ignores the question of identification. Such a view can be crudely described (for a more detailed description, see the articles cited under note 4) in a single sentence: our entire sensation discourse, at least in its descriptive and explanatory roles, could in principle be replaced by descriptions and explanations that referred solely to brain processes. To get an intuitive grasp upon the notion of replaceability, imagine an advanced society which has a developed psychophysiology. In this society children, when burned, cut, pricked, kicked, suffering from headaches or influenza, are taught, not the concepts of 'pain' and 'hurting', but rather the concepts of (say) 'C-fibre firing', or 'rapid irregular D-fibre firing'. They learn to tiptoe quietly around their father when told that his C-fibres are firing — what we would call a hangover; and if they require consolation and attention, cry 'It's firing, it's firing' instead of 'It hurts, it hurts' (the unfamiliar often sounds absurd). The point is that the descriptive and reporting functions of such a language need differ in no important respects from those same functions fulfilled by our use of 'pain' and 'hurting'; and I see no reason to suppose that other uses to which we put our pain terminology, such as seeking or expressing sympathy, warning, and the like, need not be fulfilled too — but of course this does not concern the physicalist. Certainly we should freely admit that there may be no one-to-one correlation between what we identify as pains of various kinds, and the brain states individuated by this hypothetical society; it may frequently happen that a term like our 'headache' is replaced by references to two or more distinct brain states, and, conversely, what we in our society regard as different pains may be more suitably treated there as a single brain state. This is immaterial; for we already know that psychophysiology cannot be tied down to our mental ontology. One cannot object to this hypothesis that the members of the advanced society simply lack experiences which we, in ours, have. They have just the same range of experience, but describe and report upon it in different terms. Moreover, their reports would be just as non-inferential and immediate as ours are. In fact even today we find a faint shadow of this sort of non-inferential reporting upon states of the brain; subjects can be trained to report upon the presence of alpha-wave activity in the brain. These reports are non-inferential and immediate, and are reports upon alpha waves, nothing less. nothing less.

Eliminative materialism has indeed all the advantages of theft over honest toil; but our physicalist can contend that the honest toil is honestly misplaced. All that he requires is that it should be possible in principle – he can cheerfully admit the impossibility in practice – for such a wholesale replacement of pain discourse by brain-process discourse to come about. So long as this is agreed to be logically possible, he is entitled to say that pains just are brain processes, much as a physicist may say that tables are nothing over and above clouds of molecules, without in any way advocating an end to talk of tables.

This, then, is how physicalism should deal with sensations; and there is an interesting consequence of this method of treatment. We find that sensations are no longer intransitive, but have become transitive, states – for the physicalist has equated the sensation of pain with the process of detecting bodily damage and malfunctioning. So we arrive well-prepared for the broader discussion of transitive conscious experiences, a class far larger than the class of sensations, and hence much more important; and, moreover, a class which now proves to include them. We must now tackle the question of consciousness head-on; but fortunately our examination of pain above can be adapted to illuminate the trickier notion.

'There is no need to discuss what is to be called conscious: it is removed from all doubt.' So claimed Freud;[5] but William James remarked, 'I believe that "consciousness" is the name of a nonentity, and has no right to a place among first principles.'[6] Presumably, on the basis of the remarks made earlier about the ontological status of the mental, I need not spend time here arguing against the thesis that 'consciousness' must be either a mental *entity*, or an *act* of the mind, or a *property* of the mind, or anything else of specific ontological status – we need not return to ontological absolutism. There being, then, no legitimate answer to the question 'What sort of thing *is* consciousness?', we can move straight on to the question that we found so profitable when dealing with pain: 'Under what conditions, to what, and why, do we ascribe consciousness?'

James again: 'The study *a posteriori* of the distribution of consciousness shows it to be exactly such as we might expect in an organ added for the sake of steering a nervous system grown too complex to regulate itself.'[7] This remark evidently accords well with the earlier treatment of pain; and indeed, since pain is a form of consciousness, we should expect that the grounds upon which we ascribed the capacity for pain will be of the same kind as those on the basis of which we ascribe consciousness in general. There are degrees of consciousness; for, following James's hint, some creatures need none, and most need less than do humans – and in humans the amount of consciousness may vary. Consider the frog. It catches enough flies to live on because the retinal irradiations from small moving black objects trigger off its tongue-flicking reflex. Is it conscious of the flies it catches? It would starve if surrounded by inert flies. It would seem that in so far as we are reluctant to say of the frog that it is conscious of the flies, this is because we know that the tongue-flicking reaction is an automatic, wired-in reflex – inflexible and rigid, a reaction that cannot be modified to meet altered circumstances – again like the human patellar reflex. Now a frog has a meagre and restricted sensory field; it registers a world that is simple and stereotyped, and its range of reaction to the registered stimuli is correspondingly limited: it needs no more. By contrast, a dog that chases a cat does seem to be conscious of the cat; and the reason we are willing to say this is because we believe that instead of chasing the cat he could have ignored it, pretended to ignore it, growled, barked, or gone to sleep. Moreover, other things discriminated by his senses at the time (his master about to go for a walk, his dinner dish, a rat, a thunderclap) could complicate, and cause him to modify, his initial reaction. A dog experiences a much richer and more diverse sensory field than does the frog (which is again to say that its neural chains fire to a greater number of types of incoming stimuli), and so it must have a far greater repertoire of action and reaction, reaction that can be adopted to suit fine distinctions in the incoming stimuli.

So, still following the pattern of the discussion of pain, we can say that the more a reaction looks to us to be a genetically endowed or conditioned response, the less willing we are to call it a conscious reaction. We need to find the capacity for selective response, the capacity for discriminative behaviour; which means that the animal must be able to adopt, adapt, modify, learn, and reject reaction strategies to diverse stimuli. If all, or virtually all, human behaviour consisted of genetically pre-wired, specific reactions to specific stimuli — all, that is, like the frog's tongue-flicking or the patellar reflex — then we could not be called conscious. Novelties in the environment would reduce the possibility of survival to mere chance, as there could be no provision for coping with situations of a new kind; indeed, we could not be said to recognise such novelties. On the other hand, when we find the ability to act and react in new and flexible ways, appropriate to a variety of situations in a rich environment, then I suggest we call the creature conscious, and its discriminations conscious discriminations.

The ascriptions that this account explains accord with our intuitive beliefs. We can be more or less stringent about the degree of flexibility and diversity to be found in behaviour, until we reach a mean at which the creatures we intuitively believe to be conscious do get included in the category of conscious beings, and the rest not; we can attribute consciousness to many animals without becoming vegetarians — for they may have little consciousness, and little capacity for pain. The greater the need for consciousness, the more we shall find.

We notice graduations of consciousness in our own experience: in a dreamless sleep we are conscious of nothing, react to nothing – are unconscious.[8] If barely awake, we do react to a few stimuli: we might stir to move a foot further away from a hot fire, or turn the head away from too bright a light, but little more. Meagre discriminations, meagre reactions; and meagre consciousness. In normal wakeful conditions we discriminate a good deal, and are capable of all sorts of reactions; and then there are states of heightened consciousness, when we are aware of countless small details, sensitive to fine variations in the sensory field. Dangerous situations can evoke this high-keyed consciousness, which fits the thesis that we have the degree of consciousness that we need; so can drugs; but even without danger or drugs it is fairly common. As well as all this, there is a more sophisticated and refined mode of consciousness, in which what we are conscious of are not external objects but rather some of our own psychological processes; the stimuli of which we are conscious, in other words, need not all be produced from the external world or by kinaesthetic perception, but may arise from processes in the brain, for example when items are recalled from the memory. Our response to such stimuli need not consist of overt physical activity, but can consist of thought and reflection, another sort of purposive behaviour.

Consciousness on this account emerges as an explanatory notion, which is just what we should expect a physicalist to make of it. If a creature is so constituted as to have numerous goals and sub-goals, and if its behaviour is a function of a wide range of sensory stimuli, of its stored information, and of a weighted complex of present and longer-term goals, then we call it conscious, because we call its discriminations and reactions conscious discriminations and reactions. We are explaining, by appeal to this capacity for sophistication and flexibility, what we would be unable to explain adequately by supposing automatic and reflex reactions to stimuli: we have to account for selective response. This ability to discriminate consciously is a biological necessity. If a creature is to thrive in a rich and changeable environment, a creature with a number of needs, aims, dangers, and interests, its actions and reactions must be flexible. One goal needs to be subordinated to another, long-term ends pursued by various means, action-routines must be learned, modified, or discarded in response to altering or unforeseen circumstances, and goals themselves adapted or abandoned. Non-conscious reactions, on the other hand, are inflexible patterns of activity triggered off by few and specific stimuli; these suffice for rudimentary organisms with few and simple needs, whose sparse environment allows them to thrive with reflex and automatic responses to determinate stimuli. Human beings have some such reflexes from birth, and may come to acquire many others as conditioned responses (e.g. the reaction of changing gear when approaching a steep hill in a car, or that of grabbing for a falling piece of Dresden). The conditioned responses save time and attention, for they allow us to perform without conscious attention countless routine chores. Most ordinary machines, however complex their behaviour, have their outputs determined uniquely by codified inputs, and so could not be called conscious.

None of this is in principle immune to a functional analysis. We are not asking the neurophysiologist to discover a cerebral correlate for 'the thing which is consciousness', since we have denied the need to talk in those terms. Instead, we ask of the psychophysiologist an increased complexity and richness in the type of cerebral structures and functions he postulates to explain sophisticated human behaviour. Whereas a functional analysis of such an automatic reaction as the flick of a frog's tongue when a fly flies before it may need only to postulate (as

its most global *r*'s) an input-processing mechanism and a
selector mechanism that operates upon the restricted range of
bodily movements open to that animal, an analysis of human
conscious behaviour will need far more. For, *inter alia*, and
again treating only the most global *r*'s, there will need to be
such items as: processes that compare interpreted stimulus
inputs with information 'bits' retrieved from the information
store; processes to perform this retrieval; processes that rank,
in order, short- and long-term goals, given the environmental
information; processes to overrule the choice of one action-
routine in favour of another if the environment or the
preferential ranking of goals is altered; processes to scan lower-
order cerebral systems in order to modify their operations in the
light of data coming in from negative-feedback processes ... and
so on and so forth. Despite the daunting and formidable complexity of such a task, research along these lines proceeds apace.[9]

In sum, to discover such cerebral processes, to find their
structural realisations, and to understand their workings, is to
provide the physical basis of consciousness. Certainly this
conclusion will leave many unconvinced and wanting to say
that consciousness must be something more than I have
allowed. In the next chapter we shall see that the Greeks
seemed to manage splendidly without any notion equivalent to
consciousness; but to conclude this one I shall argue that the
above thesis is sufficient to explain all our attributions of the
term.

Consider, first, an intuitively plausible objection.
'Consciousness must be something more than the capacity for
flexible and modifiable behaviour: it is easy to imagine a group
of entities, human in appearance, physiologically structured
just as we are, and behaving just as we do, but who are
nevertheless non-conscious – a zombie community, who never
experience pain, love, or fear, no matter what their actions may

be, no matter what sorts of physical processes go on in their heads.' (This is an inversion of the Cartesian thought-experiment that a person might be bodiless: these zombies are mindless.)

Let us take this fantasy seriously, and suppose that we are studying the zombie community as visiting psychologists. We examine and observe their behaviour, and begin our description of their behaviour with (relatively innocuous) psychological terms: they hear, speak, see, learn languages, and so on. We would have no reason to deny them these predicates, for the criteria of attribution are fulfilled (by hypothesis) to precisely the same extent as they are with our fellow-men. To discriminate certain wavelengths of light rays by means of an organ which is indistinguishable from the eye simply *is* to see. After a more prolonged scrutiny of the zombie community, as they become better known to us, we find that to explain their behaviour we must have recourse to predicates such as 'hopes', 'remembers', 'likes', 'dislikes', 'fears', 'expects' – again because their behaviour is *ex hypothesi* the same as that of humans, for the explanation of which, in ordinary-language terms, such predicates are indispensable. We have not been driven to ascribe *sensations* of fear yet; but with Wittgenstein one can claim that reference to phenomenal sensations is inessential for the correct ascription of states like fear. More detailed study of the zombies may find us calling some self-deceived, others strong-willed, others yet suffering from paranoiac tendencies, and so forth.

But as we continue to fill out our description of the zombies' behaviour, the self-imposed hypothesis that they are not conscious will create greater and greater difficulty. For many predicates we must refuse to apply if the hypothesis is to be respected, since to attribute predicates of a certain kind implies, weakly or strongly, that we are dealing with conscious creatures. Evidently we cannot say that they are aware of something. But no more is it legitimate to say that they notice, apprehend, attend, understand, or are embarrassed. This is a matter of conceptual interdependence; the vocabulary of psychological terms forms an interlocked web — a fact that was noted in the discussion of the ascription of beliefs and desires — the terms of which have multiple links with one another. One cannot regard 'being conscious' as analogous to one of many spikes on a hedgehog's back, a spike it might have or lose independently of all the other spikes. Being conscious is conceptually bound up — such is the way our mentalistic vocabulary is structured — in a web of further psychological terms, particularly with such terms as 'notices', 'attends', 'is embarrassed', 'conjectures', and many others. These in turn are linked to further, different concepts, such as 'sees', 'hears', 'believes', 'wants', 'fears', or 'thinks'. Such contextual implications amongst our mental concepts govern the selection of descriptive expressions we bring to bear; and the more psychological terms we ascribe to any entity, the more become applicable through these implications.

In short, there can be no cut-off point at which we can divide mental predicates into two kinds, those that do and those that do not imply consciousness. Consciousness, a matter of degree, is not so simply entailed or not entailed as this; and a sufficient number of predicates of what might seem to be the first kind will presuppose that many of the second kind are applicable — such is the consequence of having a web of concepts. I am not, of course, saying that once we have attributed any set of psychological terms to an entity we are thereby committed to giving it the whole lot. That would be absurd; the contextual implications and connections linking mental concepts are sufficiently loose and detachable for us to ascribe, if we have to, stringently restricted sets to computers, dogs, the mentally retarded, infants, and so on. I am saying rather that we cannot ascribe all our psychological terms *bar one*; the meaning of a psychological term is not learned only through behaviour (pain behaviour teaching us how to apply 'is in pain') but is learned also through a grasp of its connections with related terms (for pain, concepts such as pity, dislike and fear, hurting, remedy).

It is instructive to compare 'being conscious' with 'being intelligent'. Once one has described in some detail the intellectual achievements of someone over a wide range of activities, if all are performed to a high standard, then to deny he is intelligent signifies a failure to grasp what 'being intelligent' is. There is no room for the possibility that some new and deep evidence, unrelated to intellectual performance, might turn up to refute our earlier judgment of him as intelligent; performing to a high standard over a sufficiently wide range of intellectual and practical tasks just is to be intelligent. Each individual item of supportive evidence is not *per se* proof of intelligence, but rather of competence at task T $(T_1, T_2, \ldots T_n)$; but competence at enough diverse T's constitutes intelligence. So, too, with consciousness. There is no unique bit of evidence which, alone, proves or disproves the statement that some entity is conscious. But various kinds of behaviour justify our attributing predicates F, G, H, ... , to that entity; and many of the predicates F, G, and H (etc.) are such that to possess enough of them adds up to possessing consciousness. As with intelligence, there is no possibility that new and deeper evidence might appear to alter the validity of the ascription of consciousness. Both intelligence and consciousness ride pick-a-back upon sets of testably ascribable predicates, and are swept along with them as a simple matter of our linguistic practices and the structure of our mental vocabulary. One could say that they were 'second-order' concepts, or that they operated as it were adverbially, describing the ways in which other mental concepts relate to each other and to behaviour.

In conclusion, the two sides of the mind-body debate can be merged together in physicalism, if we add a touch of Eliminative Materialism. Sentience is a phenomenon that can be given the same treatment as sapience; and it is no less amenable to correlation with neurophysiology.

Notes

1 'Privacy', in A.J. Ayer, *The Concept of a Person and Other Essays* (London, 1964), pp. 52–81.

2 See, for example, L. Watson, *Supernature* (London, 1973), p. 223.

3 D.C. Dennett offers a helpful definition of two kinds of awareness in *Content and Consciousness* (London, 1969), pp. 118–19; it is criticised and amended by R. Rorty in 'Dennett on Awareness', *Philosophical Studies*, XXIII (1972), pp. 153–62.

4 Eliminative Materialism is described and defended by R. Rorty, in 'Mind-Body Identity, Privacy, and Categories', *Review of Metaphysics*, XIX (1965), pp. 24–54. It is attacked by J. Cornman, 'On the Elimination of "Sensations" and Sensations', *Review of Metaphysics*, XXII (1968), pp. 15–35; Rorty has replied with 'In Defense of Eliminative Materialism', *Review of Metaphysics*, XXIV (1970), pp. 112–21.

5 S. Freud, *New Introductory Lectures on Psychoanalysis*, College Edition, ed. and tr. J. Strachey (New York, 1964), p. 70.

6 W. James, *Essays in Radical Empiricism*, ed. R.B. Perry (London, 1912), p. 2.

7 W. James, *The Principles of Psychology* (New York, 1890), vol. I, p. 144.

8 There are apparent counter-examples to this which I shall not discuss, such as the puzzling phenomena of sleep-walking and epileptic automatism. These could be shown to fit the general theory, but an adequate defence of this claim would take us too far afield.

9 See for example D.M. MacKay, 'Cerebral Organization and the

Conscious Control of Action', in J:C. Eccles (ed.), *Brain and Conscious Experience* (New York, 1966), pp. 422–45; R.W. Sperry, 'Neurology and the Mind-Brain Problem, *American Scientist*, XL (1952), pp. 291–312, and 'Towards a Theory of Mind', *Proceedings of the National Academy of Science*, LXIII (1969), pp. 230–1.

CHAPTER 7

MIND UNDERMINED

I F the foregoing arguments are valid, the physicalist we have described has no longer to contend with 'the mind-body problem'. The problem, though, is dissolved rather than solved: psychophysiological functionalism prevents it from arising, stops the question even being posed. The reason, very simply, is that it allows for no class of mental events, states, or processes that can be set in any interestingly problematic relation to a class of physical events, states, and processes. For the traditional category of 'mental events' can be divided into two kinds. One kind comprises the items picked out by the everyday mental terms of common idiom; and these are irrelevant to the question of the relation between the sciences of psychology and neurophysiology. Alternatively there is the other kind, items picked out by terms that are capable of playing a part in the conceptual apparatus of psychology; but *these* items are no longer events, states, or processes that can be contrasted with, or set in opposition to, the events, states, and processes of neurophysiological theory. Instead they belong firmly and ineliminably to the molar levels of a single and unitary science of psychophysiology, a science unified by the 'Chinese boxes' methodology of functionalism. From this science no tier or 'box' can be removed, nor can it be reduced to or identified with any other 'box', without destroying the whole interlocked structure. The labels 'mental', and 'physical' have no part to play in the description of this science; and the labels 'psychological' and 'neurophysiological' mark nothing more than a pragmatic and often convenient way of distinguishing the clearly molar level from the clearly micro-level of the hierarchy. In short, this physicalism declares the mind-body problem to be a pseudo-problem. Such a conclusion will be better understood, and perhaps found more palatable, if we take a quick look at philosophical psychology before 'the problem' arose, and then glance at the arguments that gave birth to, and nourished to full growth, the mind-body dualism.

Aristotle was not troubled by a mind-body dualism. Certainly in his psychological works he does provide an answer to *a* form of dualism, that between *psuche* and body; but this dualism, which arose with the Presocratics and with which both Plato and Aristotle wrested, does not run parallel with our mind-body, mental-physical, dichotomies. The term '*psuche*' cannot be translated as 'mind'[1] – even though, as we shall see, the *psuche* can most profitably be compared and contrasted with the mind. Aristotle (and all Greek philosophers before him) lacked the concept of 'a mind', and would not have wanted it had it been explained to them; lacking any such notion, they lacked, too, the concept of 'the mental'; and hence they had no mind-body problem. Within Aristotle's psychology the question of the relation of mental to physical cannot even be posed (though this has not prevented philosophers from attempting to pose it), just as within a functionalist physicalism the question can no longer arise. What justifies the 'just as' of the previous sentence is the fact that Aristotle's psychology is an ancestor of the functionalist methodology described above, as a very brief sketch of his thesis in the *De Anima* [2] will make clear. (In this short outline, I shall deliberately ignore the one outstandingly difficult dualism of the work, that between the active and the passive intellect (430a 10 – a 25). Such neglect is pardonable because this dichotomy is not essential to Aristotle's psychological theory – indeed it obscures an otherwise clear and convincing account – but it is rather imposed upon his psychology by his ethical, theological, and metaphysical preoccupations. If we detach his psychology from these other strands, we can legitimately enough pretend that for Aristotle both active and passive intellects are part of a single capacity for rationality – as I believe he would himself have held had he been concerned with psychology alone.)

Aristotle describes the relation of *psuche* to body as that of form to matter (412a 6 – 413a 10); the *psuche* is the form and 'first actuality' of the human body. He calls it the 'first' actuality because to describe the human *psuche* is to describe the capacities that a man characteristically possesses; the occasions of acting in accordance with any such capacity constitute the second actuality, wherein man exercises these powers. So the *psuche*, like all forms, gives the 'what it is to be' a human being – to be a person is to be an entity that can engage in the activities specified by the description of the *psuche*. The capacities in question include some that we share with plants or animals, such as the ability to absorb nourishment, to move, and to exercise all five senses; but humans have, too, a further power that animals do not have: they can reason. Reasoning is divided into two kinds – practical reason, a uniquely human possession, and contemplative or speculative reason, a faculty shared with the gods. Aristotle's 'reason' or 'thought' (*nous*, *noesis*) we should think of as comprising our notions of reason, thought, intuition, deductive and inductive inference, speculation, theorising, and so on.

Not all forms of things are *psuchai*. A form that is a *psuche* differs from one that is not, in that a *psuche*-form stamps the entity whose form it is as a living entity: to have life is, precisely, to have a *psuche* as form. The *psuche* is 'the first actuality of a body which has life potentially' (412a 27–8) – by actualising this potentiality it brings life. Hence a dead human body would not have a *psuche* as its form; although, since it is a substance, it will have a form (presumably its structure and design), a form that defines it as a corpse. The eye, even though it is like the person and unlike the corpse in having a form that specifies its characteristic activity (sight), does not have a *psuche*-form; and the reason is that the eye itself is not a living thing. So it has no *psuche*, but 'if the eye were an animal, sight would be its *psuche*' (412b 18–19). Like the eye are all the other functioning parts of the living organism – ears, heart, lungs, hands, the blood. The form of each of these is given by a description of its functions or characteristic activities, and the only reason this form is not a *psuche* is that none of these is itself a living creature. But (again like the human organism) the eyes, ears, hands, heart, etc., will all lose their specific forms once the person dies, as they will then no longer be able to see, hear, grasp, or beat; and they acquire another form, just as the human body at death acquires the form that defines it as a corpse. To have a different form is *eo ipso* to become a different substance, for the form defines the substance. This means that a blind eye – an eye that does not have sight as its form – is 'no longer an eye except homonymously' (412b 20–1); it is something for which we have no unique name, although we might have invented a term for it which would stand to 'seeing eye' as 'corpse' stands to 'person'.

At this stage in the outline of Aristotle's thesis it will help if we bring it into explicit parallel with the functionalist theory sketched in chapter 4. In other words, we may equate the form of a living human body – its 'first actuality', the set of its characteristic capacities – together with the forms of functioning organs or structures of the body, with the set R.

The 'second actuality', when the person exercises his *psuche* capacities, then tallies with the set G — his behavioural repertoire. The capacities specified in the description of the human *psuche* will correspond to the most global level of *r*'s in the R set; that is, they are the *r*'s that any explanation of the agent's behaviour must assign to him in order to account for his observed behaviour. The behavioural repertoire studied by Aristotle (and here he parts company with our psychophysiologist) comprises not only the activities of perceiving, thinking, and moving, but also the digestive and metabolic processes. To explain these abilities of the person, Aristotle cites further capacities (*r*'s, forms) of various organs and structures of the body, and these help to account for the more inclusive *r*'s, the *psuche* capacities. The only interesting difference we find between the two accounts so far is that Aristotle's functionalism includes what we would now call biological functionalism, and so gives a broader-reaching account of the agent, one purporting to explain *inter alia* his growth and development. But this merely indicates Aristotle's enviable ability to preserve the unity of the human sciences — and it goes without saying that biology and psychology must even today hold to the ideal of an eventual merger in the Aristotelian manner.

This very crude sketch will suffice for our purposes. Now we can drive home the essential identity between the ancient and the modern functionalist theses by running through some of the more obvious parallels between them. I begin with a couple of minor points. First, there may be no one-to-one correspondence between a capacity and a structure, any more than there needed to be between an *r* and an *x*. Certainly some *psuche* capacities may be realised directly by a complex material substance; the eye is the substance (*x*) which has the form or function (*r*) of seeing. But other capacities may need dissection into contributory capacities (r's): the capacity for thought presupposes *inter alia* the ability to store memory-images or memory-traces (*phantasmata*, distant ancestors of the engram), an ability that Aristotle assigns to the blood. The second minor point is that the only relevant substances or x's to be cited by either theory are those that fulfil a function — i.e. those substances of which the form is a characteristic activity — and are therefore substances that contribute towards the characteristic activity of the organism. Aristotle would not count as a relevant identifiable substance within his theory any item of which the form is merely a certain shape or design, rather than something specifying an ability or a function. No more would a modern neurophysiologist bother to individuate as a specific entity any group of neurons (suppose he found a group curiously arranged in a figure-eight formation) unless he had reason to believe that this complex as such played some role, fulfilled some r. In each case the ontology consists exclusively of functionally relevant items.

Third, a rather more important parallel. In either theory, whether some entity counts as a substance/an S, or whether it counts as part of the matter of a substance/an x, depends upon how it is described, and the context or purpose of the analysis. We have already seen that this is true for the modern version of functionalism; but it holds equally for Aristotle. To explain some capacity of the *psuche* — let us take the power of sight as an example — we must either find some subsidiary capacities into which the power to see can be dissected, or else we must cite some substance (or substances) of which the form (or forms) is (constitute) the ability to see. In the case of sight, we cite the substance that is the eye; the form of the eye is sight, which explains the *psuche* capacity to see. Being itself a physical substance, the eye has not only a form but also matter; and the matter of an eye is, according to Aristotle (cf. *De Sensu*,

438a 16ff.), water. If we hope to explain how the eye is capable of seeing, we must look at the constituent material element, water; this, too, is a substance (it has matter and form), and part at least of its form is its capacity to take on any colour (424a 7–10, 431a 17–18). To give this capacity as part of the form of water is to go some way towards showing how it is that the eye sees. If we persist in our request for explanation, hoping to understand how it is that the substance, water, can take on all colours, we must turn to consider its matter, searching here for constituent parts to which we can attribute forms that explain how water has the form it does have. In the *De Sensu* Aristotle does not bother to identify the constituent material parts that make up water, but it emerges clearly that the form of these constituents, whatever they may be, must include the powers of transparency and receptivity (*De Sensu*, 438b 10–11). In short, whatever physical substance we take, for it to be a substance at all it must be analysable into its form and its matter; we shall never reach 'bare' matter, for unformed matter is a logical, and not an empirical, terminus to inquiry; and so at every stage of the investigation we can sensibly treat the material parts of any substance as substances themselves, and pursue the investigation further. Thus Aristotle is committed to the view that any functioning part of an organism can itself become the subject of analysis, an *explanandum* as well as an *explanans*.

Fourth, Aristotle is no more interested than is a modern physicalist in defending an identity theory between psychological and physiological processes. Indeed, his sophisticated functionalism must debar him from making any such identifications, just as functionalism debars a contemporary psychophysiologist from identifying, say, information-storing with information-storing mechanisms: it is as straightforward a category-mistake to equate matter with form as it is to equate a structure with a function. In other words, we should ascribe to Aristotle the 'Chinese-boxes' view outlined earlier of the relation between molar psychology and (neuro)physiology (the 'neuro' must be bracketed as Aristotle had no conception of the role of cerebral structures and processes). Indeed we both can and should regard Aristotle as a monist; see, for example, the strong monistic claims at 403a 25ff., 403b 1, and 416b 33–4. But one can be a monist without being an identity theorist, and Aristotle never once slips into the error of identifying the psychological and the physiological (403a 29–b 3):

> The natural scientist and the philosopher will define each of these differently, for example what anger is. The latter, the philosopher, will call it a desire for retaliation, or something of the sort; while the former, the scientist, will define it as a surging of the blood and hot stuff around the heart. Of these definitions, one gives the matter, and the other the form and principle. For this is the principle of the thing; but it must be in such-and-such matter for it to exist.

Aristotle has occasionally been described as an identity theorist, and sometimes looseness of terminology encourages the literal interpreter to ascribe this view to him. But the truth of the matter is that he considers it so obvious that matter and form are categorically distinct, so obvious that they are not to be identified, that at times he simply does not bother to stress their non-identity.

Fifth, a particularly important parallel. In each account the subject matter is man *qua* purposively acting agent; each is trying to account for man's most characteristic and most fundamental activities. Aristotle must evidently insist upon this, since for him these capacities for action are precisely those that spell out what it is to be a person. All other capacities of a human being are subordinated to this activity; hence the only interest in *explaining* them lies in the help this would give in explaining rational purposive activity. The hierarchical structure of the abilities that constitute the *psuche* reflects the relative importance of the behaviour resulting from their exercise: thought is at the top, since it is rational activity that is the most significant and characteristic activity of a person. (Indeed in Book X of the *Nicomachean Ethics* Aristotle more or less identifies the *ergon*, the characteristic activity, of man with speculative reason alone.) The capacity to think and to act rationally presupposes the capacity for imagination, *phantasia*; this in turn requires the ability to perceive, *aisthesis*. All organisms that can perceive are able to move to or from the objects sensed; and this, as a matter of biological necessity, presupposes that these organisms can absorb nourishment and that they have adequate metabolic and circulatory processes. Each of these *psuche*-capacities itself requires the functioning of various structures in the body — the eyes, hands, stomach, and so on. So the ability to reason is the most inclusive r of all, and rational activity is the most significant g; the r that is thinking requires a ramifying descending hierarchy of subordinate r's, some of which share with it the status of *psuche*-capacities (being capacities attributable to the living organism as a whole), others of which are forms of parts of the organism. Were reason not to be at the top of the hierarchy of the creature's *psuche*-capacities, we should not be studying the behaviour of a person, but that of something else. For to lop off the top of the hierarchy, leaving only the capacity for imagination and all the powers below that, would be to find ourselves left with an animal; if the animal had human form, it would be a hairless chimpanzee. To cut off imagination, perception, and locomotion as well, would whittle the *analysandum* down to a plant; if this had human form, it would be quite literally for Aristotle what we call quasi-metaphorically a human vegetable. (The hierarchy can be whittled away only from the top because, except for the gods, each higher-order capacity presupposes the lower ones.) Whether the *analysandum* is a person, an animal, or a plant, it is the most characteristic activity, and hence its highest-order capacity, that is to be explained; and everything else is explained in terms of its contribution to that.

This means – and here we find a sixth parallel – that Aristotle's primary concern is with sapience not sentience, just like our physicalist's; sentience is required in order to explain some forms of 'sapient' behaviour – just as the capacity for pain sensation, for example, was argued to be necessary to explain the flexibility and adaptability of much avoidance behaviour. For Aristotle, sentience is required *inter alia* to explain the capacity to imagine, and that in turn is presupposed by any explanation of thinking, of rational behaviour. So for various reasons sentience must be explained; but Aristotle would strongly resist any attempt to make sense perception as significant as rationality in the analysis of a human being. In his hierarchy of capacities it comes below imagination as well as reason; and further, animals too can perceive, so this capacity cannot possibly be the most important *explanandum* for human psychology. Its explanation is but a means to a more important end.

A seventh comparison leads out of this last. We have had to analyse and attack more than once the temptation to reify mental events; and it was necessary to argue that it is the ability to ϕ (where ' ϕ ' denotes some psychological term) rather than the individual occurrences of ϕ -ing, that is the object of explanation. But Aristotle seems to have been immune to either temptation, never reifying mental events nor talking of *acts* or *occasions* of thinking or remembering. Certainly he had no conception of such 'entities' as sense data, sense impressions, and the like; this, Matson makes clear:[3]

> The difficulty is in finding a Greek equivalent for 'sensation' in the sense philosophers make it bear. It is true that in translation of *De Anima* one finds 'sensation' and 'perception' used freely where Aristotle has *aisthesis*. But this is seldom right. *Aisthesis* means 'sense' ('the five senses'), or 'sensing' (a generic term for cases of seeing, hearing, etc., individually or collectively taken ....)
>
> ... the comparatively rare formation *aisthema*, 'that which is the consequence of the activity in *aisthesis*' occurs in Aristotle's writings some ten times, and in three of these cases it is natural and perhaps inevitable to translate it by 'sensation', 'sense impression', or even 'sense datum'. All of them though, occur in the treatise *On Dreams* (460b 2, 461a 19, 461b 22), and the spooky context, the need for a word to designate a floating image not ascribable to sense perception, explains the usage.

Nor does Aristotle want to discuss occasions of thinking or desiring, or of individual memory-episodes — we no more find an ontology of the propositional attitudes than we do of sensations. Always the primary concern is with the ability to think, to desire, or to remember, rather than with specific instances of such abilities being exercised; hence he has no reason to reify any such instances into 'mental events'. Briefly, his object is not to find the physical process that is the matter of an entity of which the form is 'a desire for x'; but instead, by showing what desiring in general is (whether for x, y, or anything else), by giving its physical basis, and by specifying the form common to any desire, he aims to make clear how desire contributes to the account to be given of deliberative behaviour. Such detailed explanations of desire (and choice, anger, fear, love and hate, etc.) are given more fully in the *De Motu Animalium* and elsewhere than in the *De Anima*; in the *De Motu*, chapters 6–10, we read that the matter, the physical basis, of desire is a process of heating or cooling of a gas-like stuff which accordingly expands or contracts, thus making various other organs or bodily parts expand and contract, and eventually provoking movement of the limbs. The form of desire, about which Aristotle is less explicit, seems to be that desire must have an object (403a 27, 433a 15), and that it must always, *ceteris paribus*, lead to action – it is an efficient cause of action (*Nicomachean Ethics*, 1139a 31–2, 1147a 27–31).[4] Inasmuch as individual desires are discussed at all, it is derivatively from this general account of desiring in general. In just the same way contemporary physicalism, as we have argued, stresses the explanation not of *this* walk, but of how people can walk; not of 'a sensation of red', but of how people can and do discriminate red things; not of a thought of Vienna at t_1, but of how people can store and retrieve information about any place and at any time.

We can now justify the earlier contention that 'mind' and 'the mental' are concepts Aristotle neither has nor would wish to have. For as we use 'mind', it provides the local habitation and the name for the sum total of individual mental events – acts of thought, sense data, and the like –[5] and Aristotle has no such homeless phenomena in need of housing. Nor has he anything like the 'incorrigibility criterion' that might create a class of mental entities. He does allow that the senses have a kind of incorrigibility, at least *vis-à-vis* their special objects: 'Perception of the special objects is true, or liable to falsity to the least possible extent' (428b 18–19). But this incorrigibility is the straightforward pragmatic kind of *de facto* incorrigibility, and holds with respect to public objects – objective whiteness and hard things – not with respect to private sense impressions.

Immediacy and privacy he would regard as neither interesting nor important.[6] No; the nearest analogy to 'mind' is the *psuche*, and the analogy is far from close; the nearest analogy to 'mental' is for Aristotle the *psuche*-logical, and this is hardly analogous at all: it includes what we term the physical capacities of metabolism, nutrition, and locomotion.

The eighth parallel between Aristotelian and modern functionalism is that as well as lacking the concept of mind or the mental in terms of which the mind-body problem is stated, each version of the theory will lack the requisite notion of 'body' too. For evidently any dualist, in order to get a problem about the relation of mind and body, must have a concept of the human body as a thing that is alive, that can perform all the motions of a person, but that might or might not be the subject of psychological predicates. At the end of the last chapter the discussion of the zombie community showed this supposition of a 'neutral body' to be unreal; now, *via* Aristotle, we can see another reason why this must be so. A body that lacks a *psuche* will be a dead body, a corpse, and this won't do: the mind-body problem isn't a mind-corpse problem. So the body must have a *psuche*; and once it has that, we can examine its powers. If it neither moves nor perceives, it is a plant (perhaps oddly shaped, a human vegetable), for the *psuche* defines the creature. Again, not what the dualist requires; no more is a body-with-*psuche* that can move, perceive, take nourishment, but not reason: that is a hairless chimpanzee. But if the body-plus-*psuche* is capable of reason too, then it is, precisely, a person: the subject of *psycho*-logical predicates. In other words, Aristotle denies any distinction between 'living human body' and 'person': if it lives, it has *psuche*, and if it acts in a characteristically human way it is exercising the capacities its *psuche* assigns it, and there is nothing more to add. Contemporary functionalism will hold the same position; and indeed no other thesis is tenable,

whatever one's convictions about physicalism may be. The
very notion of a living human body that might or might not be
the subject of psychological predicates is incoherent. To strip
consciousness from a person while leaving more than a corpse
gives one an unconscious person – and that is a psychological
predication. To strip away attributions of thought and
perception leaves one with a sub-moronic person; to strip away
reason alone is to get a moron, a radically sub-human person.
With no stripping, one has a normal person. The dubiousness
of the notion of 'body' presupposed by dualism and the mind-
body problem has not been adequately examined, here or
elsewhere;[7] it would be worth the physicalist's while to attack
the coherence of that notion quite as aggressively as that of
'mind' or 'the mental'.

Now if all this is accurate – if, that is, we have indeed come
full circle, returning to a form of physicalism that is in essential
outline Aristotle's – what needs attention is not so much the
Greek neglect of the mind-body problem but rather the reasons
why we are so impressed by it. It will be instructive to leap a
few centuries and look to see how and why dualism of mind
and body was suddenly thrust upon us as a major problem.

The most striking feature of the transition from Aristotelian
monism to Cartesian dualism is its speed: we can see it done in
a couple of pages of the *Second Meditation*. Near the beginning
of the *Second Meditation* we find Descartes writing:[8]

In the first place, then, I considered myself as having a
face, arms, and all that system of bones and flesh as seen in
a corpse which I designated by the name of body. In
addition to this I considered that I was nourished, that I
walked, that I felt, and that I thought, and I referred all
these actions to the soul; but I did not stop to consider
what the soul was, or if I did stop, I imagined that it

was something extremely rare and subtle like a wind, a
flame, or an ether, which was spread through my grosser
parts.

This is a curious mixture of the Aristotelian and the pre-
Aristotelian. We begin with the body, the matter of a person: 'a
natural body that has life potentially' (412a 20–1). Then we
move on to the soul; this is given, in the right hierarchical
order, precisely those powers that Aristotle assigns to the
human *psuche*, the rational faculty subsuming the perceptive,
locomotive, and nutritive faculties. Descartes's 'soul' in this
passage is no nearer the notion of 'mind' than is Aristotle's
'*psuche*', except for one feature: it is a distinct entity, for the
influence of the Church Fathers has been at work – the soul
must, *pace* Aristotle, be a separable substance capable of
disembodied existence. So Descartes undoes Aristotle's
monism, and returns to the pre-Aristotelian *psuche*-body
dualism; and, unsurprisingly, has little idea of what kind of
substance this soul might be, and so regresses to the views of
the Presocratics – it must be a wind, a flame, or an ether,
permeating the stuff of the body. A curious conflation;
nevertheless, what is especially significant is that 'soul',
however dubious its substantial status, yet has all and only the
attributes of the Aristotelian *psuche*. Certainly, it is not 'mind',
for it still has the nutritive and locomotive powers assigned to
it.

Very shortly after this Descartes uses Augustine's method of
doubt upon the soul:[9]

Let us pass to the attributes of soul and see if there is any
one that is in me? What of nutrition and walking (the first
mentioned)? But if it is so that I have no body it is also true
that I can neither walk nor take nourishment. Another
attribute is sensation. But one cannot feel without body

.... What of thinking? I find here that thought is an
attribute that belongs to me; it alone cannot be separated
from me.

Again, it is the Aristotelian *psuche* that determines which
human capacities are to be doubted, and in which order. It is
apparently only thought that survives the ordeal. But only
apparently; for we are surprised to read, two paragraphs
further on:[10]

But what then am I? A thing which thinks. What is a
thing which thinks? It is a thing which doubts,
understands, conceives, affirms, denies, wills, refuses,
which also imagines and feels. (Italics mine.)

And elsewhere Descartes defines thought (*cogitatio*):[11]

Thought is a word that covers everything that exists in us
in such a way that we are immediately conscious of it.
Thus all the operations of will, intellect, imagination, and
of the senses are thoughts.

In brief, the four passages cited show us first a separable soul,
but a soul assigned precisely the functions that Aristotle gives
the *psuche*; then this quasi-Aristotelian soul is stripped of all its
lower functions, including sense perception, but leaving it with
thought; but then the Latin term for thought, *cogitatio*, is given
a new and extended meaning by appeal to something called
'immediate consciousness'; and so sense perception, formerly
jettisoned by the reflection 'one cannot feel without body' is
restored: 'all the operations ... of the senses are thoughts'.
Certainly what Descartes calls 'the operations of the senses' are
not what Aristotle would have called such. The *cogitatio*
involved in the visual examination of a red ball is not the
perception of a red ball, which is what for Aristotle and

untutored common sense would count as an 'operation of the senses'. The *cogitatio* is instead the seeming-to-perceive, the impression that I am perceiving something, whether I am or not; it is whatever is common to ordinary perception and a total hallucination of a red ball. Put another way, in Descartes's new usage of 'the operations of the senses', 'I think I see' counts as such an operation.

The *cogitatio* is, without doubt, one of the ancestors of the modern notion of 'the mental'; how, then, do we decide what are, and what are not, *cogitationes*? In the last passage cited above, the criterion for being a *cogitatio* is to be the object of immediate consciousness. But then, what is immediacy? The only adequate account offered, or suggested, is that we are immediately aware of all and only those things we can be incorrigible about – whatever, in fact, could base the assertion 'I exist'. And what are these? Unfortunately, they are *cogitationes*; and of these some, such as 'I am thinking', are unchallengeably modes of thought, but others are assimilated to them only by the employment of the immediacy criterion – and the circle is complete. All three of these terms – *cogitatio*, immediacy, and incorrigibility – have been given specialised meanings, but not one of these meanings can be made clear.

Worse yet: so far from clarifying the notion of a *cogitatio*, the introduction of immediate consciousness compounds its difficulties: for the relation between awareness and thought is thoroughly obscure. What is the relation between 'seeming to see' and 'being aware that I seem to see' – and is the answer to that question the same as the answer to the question what the relation is between wanting something and being aware that I want it? Sometimes Descartes regards awareness as a concomitant to the *cogitatio*, sometimes the *cogitatio* is the object of an (independent) act of awareness, and this confusion is vital:[12]

If *conscientia* adds nothing to a mental event, then it cannot be used to distinguish mental events from physical ones. If it adds to a mental event something extra, then we must consider the possibility that this extra element might be present without the appropriate mental event's being present. In that case, my having the awareness that I seem to see will be no guarantee that I do in fact seem to see ... and there will be no quietus for Cartesian doubt.

Since *conscientia*, awareness, is so unclear, we cannot say whether *cogitatio* is a kind of consciousness or an object of consciousness, an act of the mind or the object of such an act. But there is some help to be found in an examination of the no less difficult term 'idea'. This, too, wavers between being an act of consciousness and the object of such an act; ideas can be seen, like *cogitationes*, as 'operations of the intellect';[13] or 'I take the term "idea" to stand for whatever the mind is directly aware of.'[14] Over and above *this* uncertainty, ideas seem to be capacities too − a man who has the idea of God is a man who can come to know God − or they can be concepts, 'common notions'.[15] However, despite this radical shifting in Descartes's use of the term, one interpretation is avowedly more central than the rest: 'Some of my thoughts are as it were pictures of objects, and these alone are properly called ideas.'[16] Thus the notion of an idea as the *object* of an act of intellectual awareness rather than as itself the *act* of thinking, of wishing, of willing, etc., is the most central.

As for the relation of 'idea' to '*cogitatio*', a definition offered in the *Arguments* helps: 'By the word "idea", I mean the form of any thought, that form by the immediate awareness of which I am conscious of the said thought.'[17] Here 'form' is not of course the Aristotelian form, but is rather the content or topic of the thought, a non-material representation. If so, we may understand *cogitatio* to embrace both an idea and the immediate awareness of that idea. For example, if I am looking at a tree, my *cogitatio* is: seeming-to-perceive-a-tree; and this complex consists of an idea, or immaterial representation (roughly, here, sense impression) of a tree, plus the immediate awareness of this representation. Now such a model is most plausible in perceptual contexts; but for all Descartes's efforts,[18] it fits the propositional attitudes, such as fearing or willing, less well. Whatever the implausibilities or difficulties of the model, it appears that he did think that all mental activity could be analysed in terms of ideas, and the intellectual apprehension of those ideas.

I said above that *cogitatio* was one ancestor of our category of mental events; I shall now argue that were it not for the analysis of *cogitatio* into ideas-plus-awareness, we need have no mind-body dualism at all.

To defend this claim, one must show that a *cogitatio qua* act of the mind alone, simply regarded as an intellectual activity or operation, does not engender a mind-body dualism. And this simpler sense of *cogitatio* is certainly its original meaning, for it is the *act* of thinking, doubting, etc., that validates the inference in 'Cogito ergo sum'. Only *qua* idea does a *cogitatio* become an object, and then it is the object of something *not* a *cogitatio*, an act of awareness (never, Descartes insists, can a *cogitatio* be the object of another *cogitatio*). Now if Descartes had kept to the terminology of *cogitationes* alone, and had not introduced the term 'idea', we would have an epistemological dualism but not necessarily an ontological one; for *cogitationes*, as far as we know, might be physical processes. *Cogitationes* are marked by epistemological certainty, for that was their *raison d'être* in the first place; when I have a *cogitatio* I know, infallibly and directly, that I have it. This is part of the definition of a *cogitatio* (and the admitted fact that it involves a difficult and obscure notion of 'immediate awareness', with a highly problematic relation to *cogitationes*, is true but not relevant). What is important is that since the contexts are intensional, 'I know that I am thinking', and 'I do not know that any brain processes are going on in me' are perfectly compatible, and compatible too with the suggestion that thinking *is* a process in the brain. Even the operations of the senses could be analysed without postulating a mental *entity* which is apprehended by an act of the mind; for before Descartes introduced ideas into the picture, he described the *cogitationes* involved in sense perception as 'I seem to be seeing' (*putare me videre*), and not as 'I am seeing directly an inner object.' For consider how he originally justifies the inclusion of perception among *cogitationes*:[19]

> But it will be said that these phenomena are false (i.e., seeing light, hearing noises, feeling heat) and that I am dreaming. Let it be so; still it is at least quite certain that *it seems to me that* I see light, that I hear noise, and that I feel heat. That cannot be false; properly speaking it is what is in me called feeling (sentire); and used in this precise sense that is no other thing than thinking.

The italics in this quotation are mine. Descartes almost adopts what in modern jargon is called the 'adverbial' analysis of sensation − 'sensing redly' as opposed to 'having a red sense datum' − and the incorrigibility belongs to the impression that I am seeing, but not to the knowledge of any private object of perception, any sense impression. Thus even the *cogitationes* of sense perception could be physical processes; until ideas are introduced, perceiving need entail no immaterial objects. All, then, that can be derived from *cogitationes* alone is a healthy epistemological dualism (there is a real problem how we could ever know anything extra-mental), but we need as yet postulate no separable mental realm.

Ideas are quite a different matter. They are particulars; they exist; they are definitely immaterial. They cannot be identified with states of the brain, for no such state could be, for example, coloured in a chequered fashion as my idea would be when I am looking at a chess board. An idea of a bull is an immaterial representation of a real bull, and stands to a real bull as Macbeth's dagger stands to a real dagger, or as the hallucinatory rats seen by a man with delirium tremens stand to real rats. Ideas even have an analogue of spatial location; for, following the model of an inner perceiver watching a ceaseless projection of ideas on an inner screen, the mind is summoned up to give the cinema house a title. At once we have an ontological dualism to supplement the epistemological one.

It is the reification of ideas, therefore, that is primarily responsible for persuading us into the move from epistemological to ontological dualism; but it is *conscientia*, immediate awareness, that gets us to epistemological dualism in the first place. For if I am directly aware of all and only my ideas, and if all my knowledge whatever is either of, or else filtered through, ideas, it follows that nothing extra-mental or material can be known immediately. Hence the knowledge of the mental is quite distinct from the knowledge of the extra-mental. Now if we reject this notion of 'absolute' immediacy, for the reasons given in the last chapter, then we should not have epistemological dualism. For the everyday, pragmatic sense of 'immediacy' and 'incorrigibility' allows us to maintain (for example) that the knowledge that an object seen clearly in broad daylight is brown, is immediate and incorrigible. It is the quest for an 'absolute' indubitability, set in train through fear of the Cartesian doubter, that demands an equally absolute immediacy; for mediation of any sort allows in the logical possibility of error. Further, the quest for absolute incorrigibility, by foisting upon us this unanalysable

Bewusstheit überhaupt act of immediate awareness, fosters our tendency to reify immaterial ideas as mental particulars, and thereby to build up a mental ontology. If we had given 'incorrigibility' the standard everyday sense, then *cogitationes qua* acts of thought could be both physical processes and (usually) endowed with incorrigibility; it is when we are worried by the presumption that *cogitationes* must be objects of immediate and incorrigible knowledge in an absolute way that we are forced to turn to analysing them into ideas plus the immediate awareness of ideas.

Epistemological dualism and ontological dualism alike introduce the intractable problem of getting the mental and the extra-mental, the directly and the indirectly known, back together again; the sole motive for parting them in the first place was fear of the sceptic. The mind-body problem is but one part of the bifurcation imposed by foundationalist epistemology, emerging once epistemological dualism has slipped – as it almost invariably does – into ontological dualism. But philosophy has now grown out of, and rejects, faith in foundationalist theories of knowledge; the governing metaphor of our structure of empirical belief is no longer Descartes's house, built upon the firmest possible foundations, but Neurath's boat, the strength of which depends on no one part, but upon the fitting-together of all the parts. Thus we have no further motive for refusing to return from Cartesian dualism to Aristotelian monism. In so doing we rid ourselves only of problems.

Notes

1 Nor should it be translated as 'soul' – this is almost as misleading. No translation being adequate, I shall continue to use the transliterated form.

2 References from the *De Anima* will be given without the prefix '*De Anima*'.

3 W.I. Matson, 'Why Isn't the Mind-Body Problem Ancient?', in P.K. Feyerabend and J.C. Maxwell (eds), *Mind, Matter, and Method* (Minnesota, 1966), p. 101.

4 A much fuller discussion of Aristotle's physicalist theory is given by R. Sorabji, 'Body and Soul in Aristotle', *Philosophy*, 49 (1974), pp. 63–89.

5 The concept of 'a mind' is entertainingly attacked by R. Squires, 'On One's Mind', *Philosophical Quarterly*, XX (1971), pp. 347–56.

6 He often allows that one is aware of one's thoughts or memories; see 425 b 12, and *De Sensu*, 437 a 27–9, 448 a 26–8; also *Nicomachean Ethics*, 1170 a 29–b 1. But this does not license us to ascribe to him any part of the 'incorrigibility criterion'. For he argues that we are also aware that, for example, we are walking: see *Nicomachean Ethics*, 1170 a 30; and allows that we may *not* notice, or be sure of, some memories or perceptions: see *De Insomniis*, 460 b 28–461 a 8; *De Memoria*, 451 a 2–5. And finally, what awareness we do have of our sense perception is in fact awareness of a *physical* process, like the colouration of the eye-jelly; cf. 425 b 19 f.

7 It has been examined by D. C. Long, in two articles: 'The Philosophical Concept of a Human Body', *Philosophical Review*, LXXIII (1964), pp. 321–37, and 'The Bodies of Persons', *Journal of Philosophy*, LXXI (1974), pp. 291–301. I know of no other discussions.

8 All references to Descartes's works will be to the edition of E. S. Haldane and G. R. T. Ross (Cambridge, 1967), in two volumes. This passage comes from *Meditations II*, vol. I, p. 151.

9 *Ibid.*

10 *Ibid.*, p. 153.

11 *Ibid.*, *Arguments Demonstrating the Existence of God and the Distinction Between Soul and Body, Drawn up in Geometrical Fashion*, Definition 1, vol. II, p. 52.

12 A. J. P. Kenny, *Descartes: A Study of his Philosophy* (New York, 1968), pp. 76–7.

13 Descartes, *op. cit.*, *Reply to Objections IV*, vol. I, p. 105.

14 *Ibid.*, *Reply to Objections III*, vol. I, pp. 67–8.

15 *Ibid.*, *Arguments Demonstrating the Existence of God and the Distinction Between Soul and Body, Drawn up in Geometrical Fashion,* Axiom VIII, vol. II, p. 56.

16 *Ibid.*, *Meditations III,* vol. I, p. 159.

17 *Ibid.*, *Arguments Demonstrating the Existence of God and the Distinction Between Soul and Body, Drawn up in Geometrical Fashion,* Definition II, vol. II, p. 52.

18 *Ibid.*, *Reply to Objections III,* vol. I, p. 68.

19 *Ibid.*, *Meditations II,* vol. I, p. 153.

BIBLIOGRAPHY

ARISTOTLE, *De Anima*.

BORGER, R. and CIOFFI, F. (eds), *Explanation in the Behavioural Sciences* (Cambridge, 1970).

BROWN, S.C. (ed.), *Philosophy of Psychology* (London, 1974).

DENNETT, D.C. *Content and Consciousness* (London, 1969).

DESCARTES, R., *Works*, ed. and trans. by E.S. Haldane and G.R.T. Ross (Cambridge, 1967), vols I and II.

ECCLES, J.C. (ed.), *Brain and Conscious Experience* (New York, 1966).

FEIGL, H. *The 'Mental' and the 'Physical': The Essay and a Postscript* (Minnesota, 1967).

GUNDERSON, K., *Mentality and Machines* (New York, 1971).

KENNY, A.J.P., *Descartes: A Study of his Philosophy* (New York, 1968).

O'CONNOR, J. (ed.), *Modern Materialism: Readings on Mind-Body Identity* (New York, 1969).

INDEX

action: descriptions of, 10,
16–28, 44, 57–60, 65, 76;
explanations of, 10–11, 15–27,
29–30, 32, 37–42, 51–2, 60,
72–3, 76, 118, 121; types and
tokens of, 37–8, 51, 54
after-images, 6, 90
alpha waves, 90, 102
animals, 19, 58–9, 98–100,
104–8, 110, 116, 122–3, 126
Anscombe, G. E. M., 28n
aphasia, 64
Aristotle, 100, 115–27, 128,
136n
ascription of mental and
psychological terms, 52, 74–7,
109–12
awareness, 94, 95, 110, 112n,
130–1
Ayer, A. J., 5, 13n, 88, 112n

behaviourism, 9, 10–11, 18–20
belief, 5, 11, 15, 18, 21–7, 51, 73,
87, 92
body, 1, 75, 115–17, 126–7, 128
brain states, events, or processes,
10, 12, 22, 25–7, 29–30,

101–3, 106, 133
Brentano, F., 8, 13n
Bush, R. R., 66n

Castañeda, H. N., 13n
cogitatio, 129–33, 135
computers, 4, 57, 68–84 *passim*,
86, 110; artificial intelligence
(AI) computers (devices), 69,
72, 84–5n; simulation by,
68–9, 72, 77–84; simulation
(S) computers (robots), 69, 72,
77, 82, 86
conscientia, 131, 134
conscious: of animals, 104–8; of
computers, 73, 78; of people,
86, 91, 97, 103–12; states,
transitive and intransitive,
94–7, 103
consciousness, 70, 73, 94–5,
103–12 *passim*, 129–31;
degrees of, 104–6
Cornman, J., 112n

Davidson, D., 13n, 28n, 48n
Dennett, D. C., 19, 28n, 83, 85n,
112n

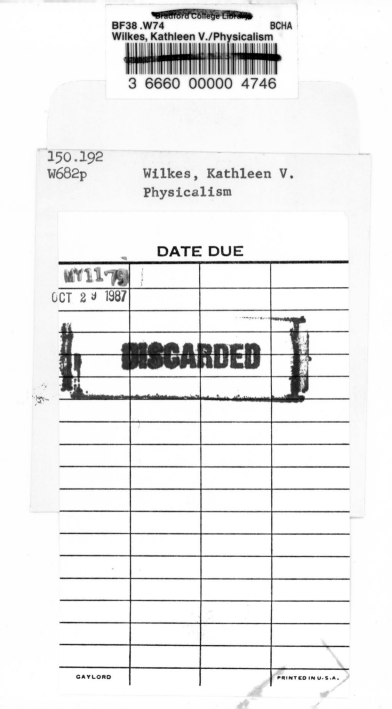